BEYOND THE LINES

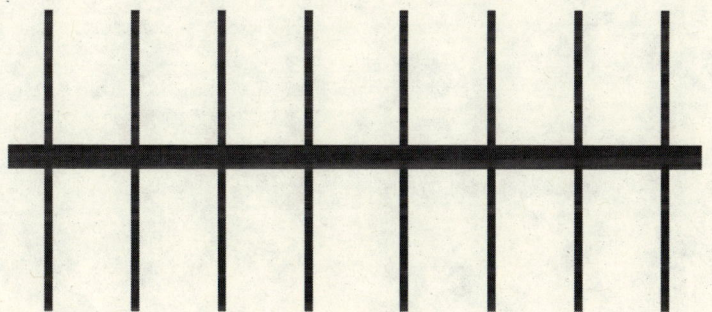

May this book
bring you many blessings!

Enjoy and thank you.

Wendy

BEYOND THE LINES

WENDY MORSE

Tate Publishing & Enterprises

Published by Tate Publishing & Enterprises, LLC
127 E. Trade Center Terrace | Mustang, Oklahoma 73064 USA
1.888.361.9473 | www.tatepublishing.com

Tate Publishing is committed to excellence in the publishing industry. The company reflects the philosophy established by the founders, based on Psalm 68:11,
"The Lord gave the word and great was the company of those who published it."

Published in the United States of America

ISBN: 978-1-61566-964-6
Family & Relationships, Abuse, Child Abuse
11.02.21

Dedication

— — — — — — —

*For all the people I know and love and all
the people they know and love…*

Acknowledgements

I thank Tate Publishing for taking a chance on this book. My family and friends demonstrated their patience and enthusiasm as I put them through my moments of doubt and numerous requests for input with wording and editing. No words can express my gratitude for the assistance of Auntie Gina, without whom this book would not be published. I thank Ben for understanding my need to write this book. And I thank the Father for being with me as He always has and always will.

Table of Contents

— — — — — — —

Foreword

In the summer of 2008 I received a call from my mother with the exciting news that her book was going to be published. This news was received with great joy in my heart, as I knew this had become a profound labor of love for her. A few minutes into my reflection on this my mood distinctly changed. How could I encourage everyone I know to read it? How could I let my life story end up in the clearance aisle of a store, in somebody's bathroom, the subject of some critic?

The answers to my fears were simple: this book is not my story though it is about me. This book is my mother's story. In this book, you will read how my mother saw our lives. You will read her heart and reflections on what it was like to watch me become the man I was going to become. You will read a journal of some of the most challenging and heartwarming moments in our journey with God. You will read them through her eyes.

My question really is: How can she let her story be on display? This is an answer I may never fully know. The fact is that she did, and the book you will leaf through, cry about, laugh with, critique, love, hate, or be indifferent to is the fruit of that decision. The courage it took her to publish this book is equivalent only to the courage it took for us to live the life encapsulated in these pages. I pray that you who are reading it will benefit from that courage.

There are times I question the boldness with which my

mother presents things. There are times I question why she left some things out, and left others in. There are times I wonder why she needed to bring *that* up. There are times I agree with what is said, and other times I do not. There are times I scarcely remember that what I am reading is about her and me. All in all, there are times I wanted her to change her mind about having it published. More importantly, however, I'm glad she has. I thank you for giving your time to read it. I thank God my mother and I made it through so that this story could be shared with others.

This story belongs to you now, also. Mom and I just lived it, but this book belongs as much to the Father as I do, as she does, and as you do.

—Ben

Introduction

For years, I have been considering writing this book about the challenges and triumphs of raising a son with special obstacles to overcome. There have been several titles and a multitude of chapter outlines. One by one, they were abandoned, and living took precedence over reflection until recently.

I went to a meeting at the counseling program where I worked and needed to park at a distance from the entrance due to construction. It was in a section of the parking lot that was beyond where the painted parking lines ended. "Beyond the Lines" would repeatedly enter my mind for the remainder of the day and into the night. Images of the lines that separate us, the lines that indicate the path a person might be expected to take in certain circumstances, or the lines within which we can expect others to live kept passing through my mind. These images allowed me to formulate the ideas for this book.

What follows is an attempt to describe and define the obstacles that faced my son and me. They would have a profound impact, both hindering and enhancing our lives together. Ultimately, we would discover the inexhaustible grace and faith that G-d (referred to from here as the Father) had bestowed upon us through these experiences and obstacles. There have been moments of fear and certainty, rage and calm, grief and hope, regret and peace. There were times when problems seemed insurmountable, but these passed quickly as our prayers and determination propelled us ever forward.

The Father provided us with numerous personal gifts, such as humor, intelligence, strength, love, and permission to not know everything (to name but a few). Where our gifts fell short of our needs, the Father provided people that knew what we needed to know, who could get us what we needed to get, and whose prayers could empower us to succeed.

We cried and laughed, had setbacks and made progress, fought (sometimes each other but mostly against those who sought to make things harder) and made peace. It was not always easy to tell when things were going well or when they were going badly. At these times, we trusted the observations and input of others to ensure we were on the right path, even at times when trusting others was the hardest thing we would ever do.

Some of the readers of this book will have experienced similar situations, others will know someone who is going through difficulties, and still others are hoping to be of use to people or families in need. Whether for you, someone you care about, or in service to others, I hope what follows will help those in need to live, as we lived, "beyond the lines."

He Belongs to the Father

It is going to hurt, they said, but it is the most promising pain. No one could tell of a certainty how long the pain would last or even when it would start, but the result would be spectacular, they said. The women in the Lamaze class were dropping like flies. This one was in labor for four hours, that one for five and a half, this one was scheduled for a cesarean. I waited patiently.

The day I went into labor was a crisp November day in Buffalo, New York. On my way home from the store, I had initiated the last left-hand turn onto our street when someone decided to pass me on the left. He came inches from hitting my car and thought it might be a good idea to get out and confront me for having the audacity to interfere with his decision to pass on a two-way side street. I thought it might be a good idea to get out and let him know that I didn't care for his decision. His female passenger noticed my condition first and covered her face. After he noticed my condition, he paused long enough for me to go on the offensive. With the yellow light of my left turning signal flashing upon us, I slammed him up against his car and demanded an apology for putting my life and the life of my unborn child in danger. When he did not respond, I slammed him again. He quickly apologized and ran to get into his car and sped off. "Thank you," I said to his rapidly retreating vehicle. Even now, I believe this was the catalyst for the start of my belated labor. Thank you again.

The first eight to ten hours were not so bad, exhausting, but not bad. As the intensity of the labor increased, several thoughts went through my mind. *Why did you eat the forbidden fruit Eve?* (To the woman He said, "I will greatly multiply your pain in child bearing; in pain you shall bring forth children" [Genesis 3:16].). *Whose idea was this natural childbirth?* (It was 1985). *Whose idea was it to have this baby in a teaching hospital where everybody and his brother could throw on a pair of rubber gloves and have a look-see?*

After twenty hours of back labor, the staff spoke to my husband about the need for a cesarean section. Our child was "sunny side up," they explained, which meant that the back of his head was pushing against my spine. I don't believe my husband fully understood as he responded that I would be disappointed if I could not deliver naturally. My baby was in distress, and I was overwhelmed. The decision was made, and I returned to my bed after doing a series of contortions during contractions in an effort to dislodge the baby.

Like those who describe seeing their lives pass before their eyes in times of extreme danger, the life I had with my husband flashed before mine. We met while working at a summer day camp in 1982. The day was very hot, and a meeting was being held to inform staff that the swimming area could not be used because of leeches. The announcement was met with groans, and he turned to me to ask, "What do you think of that?"

"Try to imagine how little I care," I replied.

"Could an electron microscope detect it?"

I just smiled and walked away.

He followed. From this, we began to speak and spend as much time together as our responsibilities allowed. We learned about each other's families, strengths, and aspirations. We experienced a strong physical attraction. We prepared ourselves for a long-distance relationship as he returned to Central Washington University to complete his degree in speech therapy, and I returned to Baldwin-Wallace College in Berea, Ohio, to complete my degree in education.

He and I spoke of our faiths and beliefs. I was actively involved in my relationship with the Father as a member of a United Methodist Church. Weekly church attendance, weekly Bible study, and daily devotions were part of my routine. At that time, I was also going to different churches and singing with a friend of mine on a regular basis. Prayer and praise for the Father's involvement in my life were important to me. My husband was not as connected with his faith heritage, Judaism. He did not go through the Bar Mitzvah process and did not attend synagogue. He said that faith was the cause of war. I told him it was the lack of faith that caused war. When people do not believe the Father is powerful enough to help us love one another, there is war. When we lack the faith to believe we deserve peace, there is war. When we lack the faith to see that the real enemy is mistrust and hate, which we must fight together, there is war. He decided that he wanted to have faith more like mine, and I was drawn even closer to him because of it.

By November of 1982, we had generated enough revenue for telephone company stocks to double in value. He returned to the East Coast for the holidays, and we spent some time with each other's families. His family lived in New Jersey and mine lived in upstate New York. While both families had some question as to how we were going to work out the differences in our faith, they encouraged us to be happy. We agreed to complete our undergraduate programs and then move to be together. We decided that the best plan would be for both of us to pursue employment. He was to graduate a few months before me, so it came as no surprise that he secured a job first, and I moved to the state of Washington in June of 1983.

Once in Washington State, we spent as much time together as we could. His job ended during the summer, as he was a speech therapist for a school system. It was difficult for me to decide what to do, as I had a degree in education but much preferred to continue the type of work I had done while in school as an assistant house parent and tutor in a group home. We took what part-time jobs we could find. He returned to full-time work in the fall, and I found part-time work as a tutor and then substitute teacher. A full-time position in a group home became available, and I accepted that while continuing to fulfill the contracts set up in the part-time work.

We still had time to get together with friends for a game night on Saturdays. While my schedule did not allow for church attendance, I did continue devotions. All other time was spent in getting to know each other and furthering our relationship.

Many friends of mine talked about their individual proposals. They were romantic stories that culminated in the person doing the proposing falling on one knee and asking, "Will you marry me?" That was not what happened to me, but I believe mine was the most romantic. During a discussion of politics, the love of my life said he nominated me to be his wife. I accepted the nomination.

The differences in our faith would result in some difficulty in the small city where we lived. We could not find anyone who would marry a Christian to a Jew. We reported our difficulty to our friends, who advised us that they could perform the marriage. Our friends were of the Bahia faith. They explained that in their faith, the second coming of the

Wendy Morse

Messiah has occurred. They were council leaders of their faith and, as such, had the authority to perform marriages. They agreed to perform the ceremony in the home of my matron of honor. The irony was not lost on us that a man whose heritage did not include the belief in the first coming of the Messiah was to be married to a woman who believed the first coming had occurred by people that believed the second coming had occurred.

On the day we were to be married, the temperature was thirty degrees below zero (that did not include wind chill factor). The pipes froze, and I needed to take a bath at the home of a neighbor. The radiator block of the engine of the best man had frozen, so he needed to be picked up and taken home. We somehow all managed to get safely to the home of our friends.

While I was getting dressed, I heard the friends that had baked our cake (a three-tiered cheesecake with Oreos as pillars) explain that they had forgotten to get a wedding piece for the top of the cake. I called out that none was necessary. Our friends took great delight in joking about what they might put on the cake. They discussed everything from hamsters to salt and pepper shakers. There is a great picture of me seeing the cake for the first time, finding Han Solo and Princess Leia action figures perched beautifully on the top. It was perfect.

Further memories flashed through my mind. There were huge memories, such as the one of my husband putting out a fire and rescuing a neighbor in the building where we lived. There were also memories of our decision to have children, move back East to be closer to family, and have my husband attend graduate school. Those memories were filled with laughter and sadness, confidence and anxiety, peace and chaos. Everything I thought I knew was about to change with the arrival of a being that would not only shape my future but also impact my perspective of my past.

The nurse's station on the nursery floor was notified to prepare my room with the things I would need following a cesarean section. The nurses with me introduced me to the anesthesiologist. While all this was happening, I felt the urge to push. I was given permission to do so, and twenty minutes later, my son was born, having turned face down when I was walking back to my bed moments earlier. No surgery needed. I was later told that the nurses in the nursery cheered when they learned we had made it.

He was not crying. He was not breathing. He could not be seen through the number of nurses and doctors feverishly working to make his first moments living moments. His dad could not decide if he should be by my side or our son's until the doctor ordered him to stay with me. The doctors had lived beyond these lines before and demonstrated a confidence that put me at ease. I knew everything would be all right because people were praying for us unceasingly. Whether he remained alive on earth or returned to the Father immediately, his purpose would be fulfilled. Then I heard him sort of humming, and a collective sigh filled the room. You see, he was not the only one who had not been breathing.

Everything went well from there. He was weighed and measured, poked and prodded, and pronounced healthy and ready for life by medical personnel. He was lifted and praised, hugged and loved, and pronounced perfect and ready for home by family. He was filled with spirit and gifts, hair counted and days numbered and pronounced pleasing by the Father.

We brought him home and began to try to put our new lives into some kind of order and balance. We did not know that this was not possible nor how much our lives had truly changed. We were dogged in our attempts to figure out a sleeping pattern, have his dad go to work rested, and complete chores around the house. Other people had made it look so easy, so either they were pretending, or we were making it harder than it should have been. It was probably a little of both.

My mother and mother-in-law came to the rescue. During my pregnancy they had warned me that parenting would not be easy. They advised me that what looked like ease in parenting was part pretence and part assigned value. They taught me the most fundamental truth: do what needs to be done now and leave the other stuff for later. After years of thinking and living almost entirely in the future—wishing I was older, wanting my career and life to start, picturing where I would be in the next five, ten, and even fifty years—I was being told to just keep my son clean and fed and let everything else go. Apart from meeting the basic needs of everyone in the house, there was nothing else that couldn't wait. Let's not forget my favorite advice: sleep when he sleeps.

My mother-in-law came to stay with us for a couple of weeks, getting up at his first peep to prepare him for me and then taking him back to his crib when we were done. She brought me food and cleaned up after us. She showed how to follow the advice she had given to do what was in front of me to do and move on to the next thing when it was time. She was gentle and loving and made sure that I was rested and ready to take on full responsibility when she left.

My mother was there to assist with keeping things in perspective. A constant beat of the same inner questions would ensure that I could keep some semblance of balance in my daily activities. The questions were: what can be done that will have the most trickle-down effect with other tasks and when? Slowly, a pattern emerged that resulted in being able to get enough sleep, complete the most necessary of tasks, and be able to enjoy what it truly meant to be his mother—using his every waking moment to interact, talking quietly, singing, laughing, and listening to his every sound in the hopes of understanding all that he was trying to convey. My favorite memory of that time was that he giggled in his sleep.

There were, of course, promises to make and keep, hopes to indulge and foster, and prayers to make and be fulfilled. Once the idea that this was a living, breathing, human being that would be here for a very long time set in, we began to see the scope of our responsibility. It was a struggle to remember what we had been taught in those early weeks. Getting caught up in future thinking can be both useful and addictive. Even more than finding balance between chores and rest was the need for balance between here and now with what if. Clearly, here and now needed the lion's share of time at this age, mingled with the knowledge that there were things that needed to be done now to ensure there would be options for the future.

Later, I would learn about the forces that interfere with a parent's warmest desires for their children. Decisions that I would make, that others would make, and that were intrinsic to my son as a person would come together at times to obliterate hope that we would accomplish good things in our son's life. Keeping faithful to a vision for his future helped us through some incredibly difficult times. I maintained my faith that the Father would accomplish much in his life.

He was too little to pray for himself. Many prayed for him in general to do well. Some were more specific, as they were close enough to us to know his needs. Family prayed with assurance that he would become all that was hoped. Prayers require movement on the part of the supplicant, and these prayers were turned into promises. When we prayed that he would be happy and healthy, there was effort on our part, such as taking him to doctor visits. I had thought getting shots when I was a child was bad, but watching them happen to my own took some getting used to. We struggled through some minor illnesses and spent the longest week of our lives waiting for results of tests to indicate whether our son had a rare and fatal disease. It turned out that all that was needed was a change in his diet. Teeth arrived, laughter abounded, and cuddling remained our favorite thing to do. Both happy and healthy were in our grasp. By ensuring that his happiness and health were important to us, he began to learn at an early age that we would then expect him to do things that ensured his own health and happiness as he became able.

Another prayer or promise made was that he would be safe. I don't think I realized how much easier it would be when he was an infant than when he got older. I chose the right car seat and installed it correctly and made sure he had nothing small enough to swallow and on which he could choke and made sure that only family members took care of him until after he was eighteen months old. There was also the safety that he would not be harmed by us. We met his needs as they arose and ensured that he would know that his safety was important to us. Our efforts to ensure his safety would result in him seeing safety as something of value that he had a right to expect and continue once old enough.

The final prayer or promise was that he would know the Father. It did not matter to me whether our son ultimately became Jewish or Christian, but I knew that he would have a connection to spiritual things. He was introduced to both faiths through traditions and celebrations. There were faith-based lullabies, storybooks, and prayers that were shared with him from the very beginning to ensure he knew of the importance of the Father in his life. Doing so also meant giving him to the Father.

There were times when he was *my* son, such as when he needed his diaper changed or a bath or to be fed. I had been taught that we all belong to the Father, and my son deserved nothing less. I had been given responsibility in his life but not for his life. His life wasn't mine to give or take. It was especially not mine to live. Everything depended on the Father's grace. Everything depended on me showing my son the way and the choices he would make for himself about following the Father once old enough to do so.

I was asked to receive him as a gift but only if I returned him. No gift this big could be carried alone. As with any gift made for me, it would receive special care. The most important prayer on my lips: "This infant belongs to the Father."

Three Strikes

Every person begins life with a set of obstacles to overcome. Some obstacles are obvious, such as blindness, severe autism, or homelessness. Other obstacles are far more subtle, such as learning disorders, mental health issues, or family problems. Our difficulties fell under the subtle category and, as such, were almost missed. Whether obvious or subtle, an obstacle remains a powerful opposing force. There were times when I knew only that there was something not right. The reminder to take care of only what was in front of me kept me moving forward even when the difficulty we faced had yet to be named. The obstacles have names now. Perhaps it is true, as in the case of Rumpelstiltskin, that there is power in a name.

One of the obstacles that we encountered in our son was Nonverbal Learning Disorder (NVLD), though we preferred learning difference. This disorder does not yet appear in the Diagnostics and Statistics Manual (DSM), which is currently in its fourth text revised edition. The diagnosis is usually given by a psychologist or neuropsychologist after IQ testing has shown a marked difference (ten points or greater) between the verbal and performance scores (with the verbal score being the higher). Other diagnoses must also be ruled out as it regards the behavioral manifestations. There are observable symptoms that can be found under other learning disorders, but when clustered in a certain way, result in the NVLD diagnosis. These symptoms include: inability to follow any task whose directions are given out of sequence (which appears to be an attention difficulty), very poor spatial relationship abilities resulting in poor motor control (which can look like hyperactivity as they fall or frequently drop things), verbal skills that surpass expected chronological ability (which can look like there is nothing wrong), and concrete understanding of language (which can look like obsessive compulsive disorder).

My son had all of these, but I didn't know the disorder existed. Not that his IQ could have been tested as a baby, however, even then we could tell that there were some difficulties. He could not walk until age eighteen months, and yet he was speaking in two- and three-word sentences. By age two and a half, a typical conversation would go something like this:

Ben: "May I have cookies for breakfast?"

Mom: "No, little boys don't have cookies for breakfast."

Ben (after getting a stuffed animal): "Puff eats cookies for breakfast."

Mom (realizing how much trouble we're in): "Nice try, but no."

Another indication was when we would give him a task where part of the direction was out of sequence. We all do this quite frequently, though I did not realize it until there was a problem. The command for someone to put his or her shoes and socks on comes readily to mind. A number of times, he put his shoes on first and then asked how the socks ended up on the inside. In our house, we needed to say, "Put your socks and shoes on." It was the same when asking him to get something. Most people would say, "Go upstairs and get a T-shirt out of your drawer." If this was said, he would go upstairs and stand in front of his dresser having heard the words *go upstairs* and *T-shirt* and *drawer* but could not unscramble the sequence on his own. In our house, you said, "Go upstairs, *open your drawer*, and get a T-shirt."

When he was three years old, he understood the language well enough to use the word *serendipity* (past, present, and future tense) correctly. Yet when I suggested it was time to sort through his toys to determine what could be kept, given away, or thrown away, I received a concrete response indicating that he saw things differently. After breakfast on a Saturday morning, I informed him that we would go through his toys and that anything he hadn't touched in the last few months could be given to those without toys. While I did the dishes, I could hear him rummaging through his toy area and thought he was getting started. Not so much. When I entered the room, there were toys spread far and wide. I asked him what he was doing, and he said, "I'm touching everything." I had said we would be giving away anything he hadn't "touched." After some explaining, we were able to get through the process without further confusion.

It wasn't until he had an IQ test toward the end of third grade that I began to get a clue about what had been happening. The results were: verbal, 156; performance, 134; full scale, 146. There was a greater than twenty-point difference between his verbal and performance IQ scores. I knew that he would not be eligible for services in an educational setting, but it was then that I began to research what this might be and what else I might expect as he got older. While more and more information did become available to us, in the early years, we mostly figured things out on our own.

We decided early on that we were dealing with a learning difference. That meant making some agreements regarding the process of learning and keeping things in perspective. We could not enlist the assistance of educators within the special education setting, given his high intellectual functioning. I was concerned that if we did not meet his educational needs in some way, he would begin to have behavioral difficulties in the classroom. This resulted in providing information to teachers as it became available to us. My mother has a master's degree in special education, and I have a bachelor's degree in education. We used our education and our knowledge about Ben's learning needs when talking to his teachers.

When we were in school we learned in sequence beginning with learning the letters of the alphabet. From there we learned that letters represented sounds that when put together were words. Words were then put together to make sentences. Sentences were then put together to make paragraphs and paragraphs made stories. When he went to school, children were taught the whole-word method which was, and is, distinctly out of sequence. Many of these children have now been diagnosed with a variety of learning differences that do not fit the whole-word method. We decided that we would re-teach him anything taught out of sequence in the classroom. Had we not been prepared to do this, I would have brought someone into our lives that could meet the need.

It then became obvious that generalizing what he had learned was equally difficult. When presented with the exact same situation, there was no difficulty. When confronted with a similar situation, he could not apply past knowledge effectively. An example was when I was teaching him not to leave things on the floor where people walked. I wanted him to understand that there was a reason there was a place for certain things. He had left his sneakers in the middle of the floor. Sneakers belong on the floor, I explained, but look what happens if someone is walking where you have left yours. This took into account his deficiency with spatial relationships, sequential learning, and understanding the reason behind things. He understood, and for the next few days, though he had been in and out several times, the sneakers were put where they belonged. Day three found the *shoes* in the path where we walked. I demonstrated the same process with the shoes as the sneakers and then asked if he could think of any other inanimate objects that could cause a problem. The process proved most useful, and I learned to put an element of generalization into whatever I was teaching.

Being able to read the nonverbal cues of others in social settings was also something that did not come easy for him. He misread seeing someone sad as that someone being disappointed in him for doing something wrong. He misinterpreted contemplation as anger. He needed constant verbal reassurance from others that he was doing all right. Watching him struggle between being gifted and quick witted in a variety of conversations while missing cues that someone was only pretending to be interested in what he was saying was confusing to me. I cannot imagine how difficult it must have been for him. I had firmly believed that there are things that are taught and things that are caught when our children are learning. It became clear that he was not going to catch on to this and would need to be taught everything.

By now you can see how tedious this could be. By the time he was four, every learning opportunity had to be sequential, had to include a way to generalize what had been learned, and needed a description of my facial expressions so that he could begin to read social cues. He was worth every moment, as are all children. I had promised that he would be happy, not sullen and overly criticized. I had promised that he would be safe, not worried that I was always finding fault. Those things were still my responsibility.

Thank the Father for humor. We found almost everything funny. Being able to laugh at ourselves allowed us to try new things, keep things in perspective, and ensure that the people near us did not get uncomfortable when something went wrong. Yelling did not happen. It was not needed. The learning difference was not something we did to each other. It was what it was. We first agreed that we would never say the word *duh*, as it was not deemed a positive, self-esteem-enhancing word. We also agreed not to laugh until both of us could see the humor. Sometimes it was just plain funny. Two of my most vivid memories came when he was older. He was twelve years old when he needed to start wearing deodorant. When I purchased it for him, I began to tell him that it is applied in the armpit. He interrupted me and said that he knew where it went. Having purchased it in winter, it would be months before I discovered that he was also applying it to his forearm, which I noticed on a day that he first wore a T-shirt. I wracked my brain for a moment trying to figure out why, and then I remembered that there had been commercials demonstrating visible versus invisible deodorants where the actors had applied the deodorant to the forearms. I explained that putting deodorant on the forearm was for demonstration purposes and that it need only be applied to the armpit. He looked at me and said that he could tell I needed to laugh and should do so before I exploded. Permission granted, I am still laughing.

The other incident was when he was seventeen years old and a senior in high school. He had been asked to write a paper and use APA style. This resulted in an expectation that he forward an outline of his plans necessitating the use of Roman numerals. He sat down at the computer, and, after starting, I noticed that he had stopped and was staring at the keys. He stared at the keys for at least fifteen minutes and then informed me that we needed a new keyboard. I asked why, and he responded that this keyboard did not have any Roman numerals on it. You must keep in mind that this was the only child in a room with mostly children that laughed with the adults when an ancient Greek child in a movie yelled, "Somebody call IX, I, I." I told him that I could tell him what people do in this situation, but he must promise that he would not get angry with himself. I then told him that the capital *I* is used for one. He stopped me as he immediately got it and said, "Duh." I reminded him of our agreement, but he said, "Yeah, Mom, but that was a duh."

The Generalized Anxiety Disorder (GAD) would rear its ugly head later in his life. This disorder is hallmarked by anxious responses that exceed the situation at hand, anxious responses where no provoking incident exists, anxious pessimism that terrible things are going to happen, and irrational thinking about how they are perceived by others and/or the source of the anxiety. This disorder does appear in the DSM IV in the mood disorder section, and the diagnostic criteria can be looked up there. Observable cues that someone is suffering from this disorder may include excessive crying, sleep difficulties, avoidance of new things or of old things that resulted in anxiety, frustration, fear, anger, and signs of panic (i.e., difficulty breathing, heavy sweating, inability to be still).

While experiencing some of these symptoms, it is very difficult for the person to have a realistic view of what it going on around him. Social cues are misread and misinterpreted. The cues are often misinterpreted as negative, and therefore the response is hostility and mistrust. There are no anxious optimists out there worrying that something good might happen. They are pessimists all.

It is difficult to tell exactly how the Generalized Anxiety and Nonverbal Learning Disorders may relate to or impact each other. Further study is necessary to determine the frequency of co-occurrence, if it is possible to have any learning difference without disordered experiences of anxiety, or if anxiety itself can produce disordered learning processes. Any way you look at it, it's a bad combination.

The disorder lay dormant for years and finally struck when he was eleven years old. Having never experienced this much pain, fear, and sadness before, he connected it with a belief that I had been killed. Later, he would tell me that there was no other way to conceive that he would hurt so badly, and his brain demanded an explanation.

There may have been earlier warning signs that he was having anxiety issues that were dismissed as something else. He had always needed to know everything that was going to happen beforehand. We often spoke of what different outcomes there could be to an event. He frequently expected the worst to happen, but it was mitigated by the fact that he felt safe when with me or other family members.

The truth is he would have had this disorder no matter what life circumstances he had. It is also true that many of the teaching skills used for the NVLD would be useful in dealing with the GAD. The groundwork of being prepared by providing information about coming events, providing clear information regarding expectations, and giving opportunities to try new things in a safe way were already how we interacted. The result would be seeing the humor in later years by observing that he "could be spontaneous as long as he knew in advance."

What was needed most was treatment. We chose a combination of counseling and medication. Also needed were a way to communicate what was happening (especially when he

Wendy Morse

was unable to speak), perspective (by both rating his levels of anxiety experiences and determining the difference between appropriately felt anxiety and disordered anxiety), and balance (making efforts to ensure that when there was a severe anxiety experience there was a corresponding hopeful experience).

Everyone we knew was informed and given information about what signs to look for and how best to respond. We treated this as we would any illness that required treatment and, as such, found that there were some who had a healing way of responding and some who would call upon assistance when needed. For this we were so grateful that so many caring people existed. This list of people was changed as needed with some coming into his life while others were moving on. With orchestration only the Father could provide, the gaps were filled seamlessly.

We learned that he experienced anxiety at various, definable, levels. The use of a Likert Scale of one to ten allowed us to rate his level of anxiety based on symptoms. An example of a Level 1 would be hair on the back of his neck standing up, a funny feeling in his stomach that could be ignored, and a mild lack of concentration. He could also have symptoms of poor concentration, difficulty sitting still, and uncontrolled crying at Level 5. At Level 10, he was unable to speak coherently, nauseated, and had difficulty breathing.

Use of the scale then gave us the means to determine a calming response plan. The responses included positive self-talk, proximity to family members, and treatment changes. For the first six weeks following his first major anxiety/panic attack, his grandmother and I shared responsibility for being with him everywhere he went. This included school, which surprised authorities but was ultimately welcomed. Other coping skills included, like with the NVLD, permission to not have to learn if it was too hard to concentrate, and we would re-teach anything that was necessary. We knew that his personal coping skills would improve as he got older, that medication and counseling would have a positive impact, and that his need for emergency response would reduce. As with any other illness, the proper level of response to an emergency situation greatly enhances the recovery process.

We also learned that "Generalized" meant just that. When anxiety came, it did not always have an identifiable source. Attaching anxiety to the situation at hand was easy to do at first. It resulted in not wanting to go swimming, avoidance of certain places, and fear of trying new things. When he was fourteen years old, he again asked permission to be excused from taking swimming class at school. Now that the emergence and immediacy of the anxiety disorder were in check, it occurred to me that we could be heading for some phobias if we didn't get some perspective. I reminded him that we knew his anxiety could attack him without provocation at any time. I told him that as far as I remembered, he began to avoid certain things because his most recent experience had included an anxiety attack. I then postulated that if he were walking across the living room, farted, and had an anxiety attack that he might start thinking that gas caused anxiety, which would not be a good thing. He was almost laughing too hard to agree to try swimming again.

One more issue would impact his life before he had a chance to truly enter the outside world. At the age of three, his dad and I decided to separate and later divorce. The decision to do so was not an easy one. As with the disorders listed above, there were a number of symptoms that the marriage was failing—mistrust, lack of shared responsibility, inappropriate comments toward each other, unexpected rages, and inexplicable grief at the loss of a relationship that ended long before the separation.

It was difficult to tell how our son took the divorce. There wasn't a lot of crying about his dad being gone, which I saw as him trusting that he would not be harmed in the process. He asked questions, but not the amount I had anticipated, given the number he was apt to ask if he observed even the simplest of things. There was no screaming or crying when he went from one home to the other. We never used the term *visitation*, as it suggested that he did not belong equally at both homes.

From an early age, it was apparent that taking care of others was something that was part of who he was. Perhaps he kept his thoughts to himself as a way of taking care of us, seeing as how we were both struggling. Perhaps it was the beginning of an understanding that there were things in this world for which there were no easy answers. Maybe the depth of his experience with this change defied his being able to put into words. Whatever the reason, I look back on this change in our lives as something we all worked on together, putting more effort into it because we wanted it more than we wanted to be together.

He remained in my custody with liberal time between one home and the other and shared responsibility for medical and educational needs. Most of the responses to the NVLD and GAD were mine to do, and after I found something that worked, I passed the information on to his dad so there would be continuity of response. This was not always easy to accomplish, and I will spare the sordid details of the ways divorced people can be toward each other, but for the most part, we were able to follow a path that would ensure the greatest likelihood of success.

Having all of the above issues to deal with could have determined the path his life would take. Carefully laid out lines of direction are associated with any one of the above. When a child has a learning difference, he will need special education services. Behavior problems can be expected as he struggles through the usual educational environment. Chances are higher that the parents suffered from the same limitations and had no desire to be actively involved in the child's educational experience. He would be expected to drop out or get a high school equivalency diploma. He would probably move from job to job and struggle throughout adulthood with tasks that most adults take for granted as coming easily. Have you heard or thought any of these?

When a child has a diagnosed mental illness, he can be unpredictable and difficult to be around. Only family, mental health professionals, and programs that have specially trained staff can provide adequate supervision or care. If the child has to go into the hospital for mental health treatment, it is something to be kept secret even though neighbors bring a casserole to your house in the event that your child breaks a leg. Having a mental health diagnosis means you are weak and unable to take care of yourself. For your entire life, you will need to be careful in public lest someone notice your deficiency and demand that someone do something about you before you attack one of their family members. (I here acknowledge that this is necessary in *rare* occasions.) Have you heard or thought any of these?

Being the product of divorce holds no greater hope. The children of divorced parents are more likely to be violent, have problems in school, become involved with the legal system, and become involved with drugs. They have more difficulty with socialization and have more difficulty making and keeping friends. Children of divorce spend more time in day care, more time watching television, and more time in isolating activities such as video games and solitary play. They are more likely to take on adult roles in the home and become the arbitrators of their parents' selfish difficulties. Have you heard or thought any of these?

There are some truisms in the above statements. I too have watched many children and families struggle with making sure that they do not become statistics. Not every person experiences what is expected. None of us need follow any path, line, or direction that someone else determines. Our family believed in endless possibilities, which brought both promise and dread. We believed that he could, and would, accomplish anything of his choosing. We believed that the Father had a hand in all of the good things that would come his way. We believed that: "this baby belongs to the Father."

Abuse

— — — — — — —

Ben was in day care before his dad moved out. It was a nice, unassuming place in the basement of a nearby church. The decision was easy to make after taking a look at a few places. The staff and director seemed competent. The place was clean with signs of children having a good time. He had a wonderful time in the first one and a half years. He progressed from one group to another and made the transition smoothly. The only glitches were that they did not like him being in cloth diapers until two and a half, and he had a prankster streak in him.

On several occasions, his teacher would need to speak to me when I arrived to pick him up. On one of those occasions, he had convinced all of his classmates to paint one another red when working on a fridge box house. On another, he had convinced everyone to take their shoes and socks off and mix match one another's socks. On any of the occasions when the teacher returned to the room to find the difficulty, she would ask, "Whose idea was this?" everyone pointed to my son, and he would smile and shrug. The stories were told with the humor they deserved and an agreement to take the boy with her whenever she left the room was finally made.

He was three years old when his dad moved out. This prompted my need to drop him off at the center earlier than usual. This also prompted a special request to do so, as there was only one staff person working in the half hour before the rest of the staff arrived. He was one of a half dozen children attending the center at that time. His attitude changed dramatically toward the place a month after early drop-off began. He said he didn't want to go or would actually cry when dropped off, something he had not done since the first day. I began to notice that other children were experiencing the same thing.

Looking back, it had been too easy to dismiss the issue. He was not seeing his dad every day, he was more tired at the early hour, and he did not spend as much time with me in the evening due to going to bed earlier. I had even dismissed it as discussions began about going to prekindergarten in the fall might be making him miss the place before he left.

Then he started to have bathroom issues. This was followed by crying more easily, insisting doors be locked, and pulling me into a room to say he had a secret that he couldn't tell me. On his last day at the center, he had begun to cry. One of the other parents observed that "it was his turn to cry." Then it hit me, after six months of my son's agony, that something was very wrong. I grabbed him, everything that belonged to him, and advised the only staff person there that he would not be returning to the place until I found out what was going on.

We spent a day together during which I told him that he and I would be alone together for however long it took for him to be able to talk about what had been happening to him. He said he couldn't tell me. He explained that they had told him that his dad knew and that was why he had moved out and that I would leave him if I knew. They told him I wouldn't believe him over the adults. They told him they would kill me if he told.

I assured him that none of this was true and that it took a lot of courage for him to give me the clues that he did. I told him that I was sorry it took so long for me to figure it out. I told him that he would need to go to the hospital for a checkup after he described some of the things that were done to him.

While at the hospital, he explained some more of what happened, and I was told that there was evidence that he had been abused but nothing that could be collected to use later. He made it clear that it was not a family member but could not bring himself to say who had done it other than that there was more than one. I was sure that they were at the day care center but only knew of the one teacher.

Hospital staff had called Crisis Services, and they were wonderful. They had also called Child Protective Services and the Sex Offense Squad. They had nothing but a barrage of questions. He answered logically and with consistency to every question asked. He was poised, specific, and remembered enough details for authorities to move forward if he would only tell us who.

Counseling began as soon as possible with the assistance of Crisis Services and the Crime Victim's Board. With the help of his counselor, he was finally able to say who they were. It turns out that the morning staff person's father worked as a janitor for the church, and it was father and daughter that together perpetrated a number of sexual offenses against the children.

Authorities were notified again, questions were asked again, and he was clear and precise again. He was called to the Sex Offense Squad to speak with various detectives and authorities. These included members of the district attorney's office, who agreed that even at this young age his testimony would be admissible if they could get more evidence. After one of these interviews, he and I were leaving and talking about what everyone wanted of him. He looked up at me and asked, "Don't they know it's over?" We walked back to the official and let him know it was over, that my son had not had any control over what had happened to him, and he would have control over this. I went on to say that my son already knew too much about what adults could do to children, and he did not also need to see a flawed legal system fail to bring any justice.

He was a child and had a child's concrete understanding of right and wrong. To put him through any further telling and retelling of the story when authorities clearly had no intention of moving forward seemed idiotic at best. "Feel free to contact me if you get anything else" were my last words to them. I did not hear from them again.

Once feeling safe, he began to share more about what happened to him physically and emotionally. He asked me if it was alright for someone "to drink his pee-pee." With every fiber of my being I wanted to scream no, but then I thought he would think he had done something wrong. With as much calm as I could muster, I would respond to all such questions with. "I'm glad you asked me that question because I know an adult has lied to you about this before. No, that doesn't have to be allowed."

On yet another occasion, he revealed to me that he had tried to protect the others by saying the abusers could do anything to him that they wanted in exchange for leaving the others alone. He told me that he was the oldest and that was his job. Later, they would use that against him by telling him that he would have to get other kids to join them so that they would leave the younger kids alone. This came out after a night terror from which he awoke crying and saying repeatedly, "I only picked the bad kids, Mommy."

There would be more terrible information to come. We would learn from others who had children there at the day care that they were never informed as to why we left. The director of the center had told Child Protective Services that the Sex Offense Squad was handling the situation and had told the Sex Offense Squad that Child Protective Services was handling the situation. The Board of Directors of the center had not been informed. The staff member in question had left abruptly on the same day we left but was allowed to return six months later. No explanation had been given to the families.

I know the question is asked about how people can get away with such things. The reason is clear, as in our case. It began with the abuse and disclosure. From there, I know that everyone believed my son. I know he was believed because the perpetrator left the scene, the hospital confirmed his story, Crisis Services moved mountains to get him into counseling immediately, authorities saw him repeatedly and agreed that his testimony, along with direct evidence, would establish guilt, and the director of the center did everything possible to cover it up. And yet nothing happened. No communication link between the investigating agencies. No continued gathering of evidence. No further telephone contact. No criminal indictments. No justice.

Post-traumatic Stress Disorder (PTSD) was added to the list of disorders he already had. This disorder has as its symptoms: anxiety; depression; anger; avoidance of certain places and activities; intense flashbacks brought on by sights, sounds, events, and/or odors; lack of concentration; and hyper vigilance. As with the obstacles listed in chapter 2, there are overlaps of symptom otology. The result was an intensity of unwanted feelings that threatened his very sanity.

The only way to combat the intensity was to direct our attention to the personal power that he possessed. One element of that power was his desire to care for others. He had told us that he had put himself in harm's way for the benefit of those younger than he. This gave him some power over the perpetrators at the time, as he manipulated and negotiated how they made some of their choices.

Another aspect of his personal power was the acknowledgment that not everything at the day care center was bad. He enjoyed and trusted many of the adults that were there. He had friends and enjoyed the activities that were available. He was able to find humor in routine activities that brought a smile to him and others.

The power of being believed and brought to safety by those that loved him had the most powerful impact of all. Knowing that he did not have to be in harm's way, that he did not have to be responsible for the damaging decisions of others, and that he did not have to fear the lies told to him by the abusers gave him power over fear, regret, and mistrust.

We "circled the wagons." No one came into our lives unless he or she was thoroughly checked and found to be safe and supportive. We returned to individual caretakers through family and friends. We took steps to ensure that he could attend the early childhood center where my mother taught first grade, which would ensure childcare from prekindergarten through second grade.

Imagine what life is like for the child that remains in harm's way. A child who is not believed or goes unnoticed remains powerless over his current situation, as well as over memories of past abuse. It is not until the child is believed, has attention paid, and is brought to safety that healing can begin to take place. Even with all the personal power we brought to bear, the recovery was painstakingly difficult. The process would impact his life in various ways throughout his developmental stages.

My many years work in the field of counseling did not prepare me for the difficulty I would have in my role as parent to a child that had been abused. Like so many others before me, I split myself so that I could be what was needed of me because being mom was too painful. When he needed an advocate, I made sure he got everything he needed. When he needed a teacher, I made sure that he was taught what he needed to learn. When he needed protection, I was his defender and guardian. "Mom" happened after he went to bed and I could call friends, family, and crisis services to cry and ask why.

The answer to the question of "why" would not be clear right away. I knew that something good needed to come of it. I knew that we would have to make that happen ourselves through prayer and determination. At some point in the future, someone's life would be touched by my son's story and the way he would overcome his adversity. These things were in the distant future.

More than any other obstacle to date, I wanted him to live beyond the lines that this event could generate. Great care and discipline would be needed to ensure that he would not be too fearful to live his life to the fullest. I taught him that the safety I had promised did not mean we could control the decisions of others, but we could learn from it and from the fact that there were far more people in his life that did not harm him. Without this lesson, he would always remain distrustful and seek to harm others before they could harm him. Most of all, he needed to learn that abuse of others cannot be mistaken for personal power so that he would not grow up and need to become a perpetrator himself.

The stakes for his success became very high. I could not have been stricter in consistency of approach. It was important to address as many, if not all, of his obstacles with every teachable moment and conversation we had. I listened for every opportunity to gently guide him away from negative thinking and faulty confusions.

Far too many issues interfered with my plan to return some balance to our lives through love, discipline, and honesty. The first interference came in the form of his dad's attempt to temper what he thought was an excess of strictness on my part. My son had just come home from spending time with his dad. I told him to take his suitcase upstairs to unpack. He responded that he had been told that he did not have to do everything I said because I was too strict. I looked at him with an unmistakable look on my face, at which point he said, "But Dad could be wrong" while he went upstairs to unpack.

Another issue that interfered with my plans was in regard to the carrying of burdens. For most of my professional career, I had taught parents that the worst thing they could do was to take on the feelings of their children. An angry child or adolescent will do something to make his parent angry. When the parent takes on the anger and begins to act on it, the child looks at her and wonders what her problem is. The child has successfully passed on the anger so it no longer exists for him. I would coach parents in this situation to say, "I'm feeling anger right now, but it doesn't belong to me. If I feel anger with you instead of you or at you, then you will still not know how to deal with it. You keep it while I teach you how to get rid of it safely."

My response to my own son at this age was different. I would use the above later in his life when needed, but now he was too young to carry the feelings he had alone, especially since they were feelings given to him by the perpetrators and did not belong to him in the first place. I took on the burden of hyper vigilance so that he would not have to. Within the pattern that I was already using to teach him things (give information in sequence, provide examples, and ensure generalization of information), I made sure there were few sudden changes or surprises to maximize trust and safety. All people assess these every waking moment without even thinking about it. When there has been an interruption in these, it is imperative to return to them as soon as possible.

By far, the largest issue that interfered with my plan that my son would experience safety as often as possible was the media. In virtually every animated movie we saw, there was a missing parent as it started or a dying parent while trying to protect his or her child. In light of my son's experience, it became important to shift the focus from the loss represented to the experience of overcoming adversity. It would have been too easy to get caught up in the losses as reminders to the threats he had endured at the hands of his abusers.

He was able to learn to see other things in these movies. As he approached age four, I had rented a movie and in it the mother of the main character dies while trying to protect him. Later in the movie, he sees what he believes to be his mother and runs toward what he sees only to discover it was his own shadow. My son asked me to stop the videotape and told me that he knew why Little Foot thought he had seen his mother. I asked him why, and he responded, "Because there is more of his mother in him than he knows."

By the time he was five years old he was quite used to a parent or parents dying in animated children's movies. In one of these, the character's uncle convinced him that he was responsible for his father's death while telling him: "Let's keep this our little secret." I watched my son's response. He sighed heavily and shook his head. After the movie, I noticed that he was closely watching the other children in the theater as we left. Once in the car, he was very quiet until I asked him what he was thinking. He told me that he could not tell exactly how many children in the theater had heard words about keeping secrets before, but they did not need to hear those words from characters in a movie. Whether it was because of the abuse or all the efforts we made despite the abuse, he would always have these incredible insights as part of his personal power.

Once a sense of safety was reinstated, it was difficult to get back to the promise that he would be happy. Almost everything was seen through the filter of past abuse in addition to the learning difference and mental health issues. Over the years, the happiness would return. At first we found happiness in the absence of things: a day without anyone getting hurt, a day without fear, a day without thinking about the past, a day without anger. It is impossible to pinpoint an exact day or time that it happened, but we finally became happy because of the presence of things. We found happiness in the presence of unrestrained laughter, the presence of the kindness in others, the presence of dreams for our future, the presence of peace. Maybe it was because we finally had the energy to see what was in front of us instead of what was behind. Maybe it was because we grew bored with the predictable responses we had to situations. Maybe it was because we had good counselors, friends, and family, who challenged us to let things go. It was probably for all those reasons, and we are grateful.

My relationship with the Father changed in the three years following the abuse. Not, as supposed, because I blamed the Father and did not think I could trust the Father. There were a few moments when I doubted that the Father cared about what happened to us, but that would require me to believe that we were somehow puppets on a string, acting out some plan the Father had for us. I do not believe this is the case. The Father made all things available to us, both wanted and unwanted. The Father gave us power to decide how we were going to handle unwanted things. Whether we chose to embrace what was bad or were adversely affected by the bad decisions of others, we would always have the power to turn away and find good. No, I was not angry with the Father.

I read and reread Romans 8:38–39: "For I am convinced that neither death, nor life, nor angels, nor principalities, nor things present, nor things to come, nor powers, nor height, nor depth, nor any other created thing, shall be able to separate us from the love of God, which is in Christ Jesus our Lord" (NASB). I firmly believe in the words of this scripture. Nothing outside of my relationship with the Father or Jesus could cause separation to occur. My prayers did not change. If anything, I went to church more often. I believed in His power to heal us and have us see good things again.

There was intense anger, to the point of rage, toward those responsible for the abuse. I believed it was possible to close off a place in my heart that I did not want the Father to see. Fear that everything I had learned about right and wrong and even forgiveness would fail me if I ever saw the perpetrators was also secreted away. Agony over why I couldn't take my son's place was yet another area I did not want the Father to touch. It did not matter that the Father knew exactly how I felt. The words of one of my favorite hymns, all but forgotten, "Oh, what peace we often forfeit, oh, what needless pain we bear, all because we do not carry *everything* to God in prayer" ("What a Friend We Have in Jesus"). The only prayer that remained: "This toddler belongs to the Father."

Safety, Control, and Trust

All of us are constantly seeking to achieve safety, control, and trust. Food, clothing, and shelter are necessary for physical health. Safety, control, and trust are necessary for emotional health. Our prayers to meet these needs are buried in other requests such as job security, confidentiality, and the ever-elusive peace of mind. The concepts are often too big to grasp but are also too necessary to ignore.

Without even realizing we are doing so, the questions of whether or not we are safe in a given situation go through our minds. We watch for broken and sharp things to avoid. We are leery of situations that have proven unsafe in the past. We are careful around people that behave in an unsafe way.

Control leads us to a similar set of questions. It is not that we need to control others. We seek instead to have self-control and watch that others and/or the situation in which we find ourselves are under control. Again, without giving it conscious thought, we try to ensure that we have control of our thoughts and feelings, that others near us are doing the same, and that we can free ourselves from any situation that has the potential to get out of control.

The last of the three is trust. Each of us is tuned in for the unexpected, paying attention to whether any change is something good. Great care is taken to ensure that others are being honest with us. It is also equally important to determine if others are going to do what they say they are going to do. An almost imperceptible assessment is taking place constantly as to whether or not we trust our own perceptions as well as trust those around us.

My son's sense of safety, control, and trust had experienced a significant interruption and needed direct and deliberate intervention to get back on track. As with all of the things we needed to relearn, we needed to take small steps and make changes slowly. In order to make sure that the interventions were deliberate, we spoke the concepts out loud and made conscious decisions and assessments. His NVLD had not gone away, so this became another opportunity to teach him specific steps and thoughts that would lead to decisions about safety, control, and trust. I would often ask him if he felt safe or in control or trusting so that he could find his own words and personal assessment tools. This could then lead to unconscious assessment as he got older.

At first, it was entirely my responsibility to make the necessary changes. New caretakers were needed. Arrangements were made so that only family members and trusted friends were responsible for taking care of my son. I could be sure that he was safe and able to talk about his memories and feelings. Each of these caretakers knew how to comfort him when needed and had the ability to report on how he was doing to ensure there would be continuity of knowledge among us. The counselor he was seeing was also kept informed.

It was very difficult to leave him with anyone in those early days following the abuse. We couldn't afford to trade one problem for another. Had he stayed only with me, he would have developed more dependence and become more anxious about any separation. I also did not want him to think that the abusers had the power to decide if we were going to live our lives as we chose.

Another step we had taken was to secure counselors for each of us. My counselor provided assistance in finding balance, grieving the loss of my son's innocence, and avoiding the power that abuse can take on through secrecy.

My son learned to put his experience into words. Words have always been his favorite thing. He found power in them and therefore increased personal power in the face of his overwhelming memories and feelings. Once we had the skills to continue to move forward, we ended counseling with the understanding that we could return at any time if needed.

We made sure that people that needed to know his story were informed, always getting permission from my son before we did so. It is his story. We made sure that everyone knew that he and I talked about everything. Every moment that we were together, we were talking. We started talking about his day from the moment I would pick him up. I cannot tell you how many times I saw children picked up in silence. Please don't get me wrong. After a day of counseling others, it was sometimes difficult to have any listening power. My son can tell you that I have had to tell him to talk if he wanted but that he might have to repeat himself as I would stop listening for short periods of time. Whether we were in the car, running errands, going for a walk, or sitting around at home, we were talking. In our words we found love, comfort, humor, strength, safety, self-control, and trust.

Steps were taken to ensure he would not become a target again. Having respect for people in authority does not mean you have to let them harm you or make you do things that are uncomfortable. Respect and vulnerability are not the same things. He learned to continue to use respectful language to authority figures and peers alike when confronted with the need to say, "No, I'm not going to do that." When he was seven years old, he was able to tell the parent of a friend that he would not watch the R-rated movie he had gotten for the children to watch for his son's birthday party in a respectful way. He was also able to use respectful language with bullies.

It should be noted that he had far more difficulty with bullies than concerns that another adult would do something to harm him again. All children have to contend with bullies. My son was the smallest and youngest in his class. He had red hair and freckles. He also had a stutter. As if this weren't bad enough, he had an overdeveloped sense of obligation to the bad kids in order to gain some relief from the memory of what he had been forced to do during the abuse. He was torn between needing to bring an abrupt halt to any bullying while remaining respectful to the bully.

After several attempts on my part to ascertain why teachers were not available to intervene, we decided to learn ways to respond. We role-played and practiced until he could be comfortable and confident responding to others that picked on him. There were times when the preparation resulted in no further bullying without a word being spoken as he carried himself differently when confident. At other times, he was grateful for the practice, as the response would come easily and with the desired effect.

In one such incident, he was participating in summer day camp. He was five years old in a group of mostly six- and seven-year-olds who were all going to enter the first grade in the fall. His group leader expressed concerns at his small size and maturity to handle being in the group. I insisted he remain in the group. She was accurate in that an older child pushed him on his first day. I was accurate about his ability to respond effectively. It was explained to me that he was toward the end of a line of children going to swimming when the older child pushed him. The push was with enough force that he bumped into the child in front of him, setting up a chain reaction that would ultimately reach the group leader. By the time she got to the end of the line to address what happened, she saw my son standing toe to toe with the child that was more than a head taller. He was patiently explaining that they did not have to like each other or even play with each other, but he was not to be touched again. He went on to say that if the child couldn't stop, he would find an adult to help him stop. The older child apologized and agreed not to do it again. There were no further incidents that summer.

Having discovered so much ourselves about learning differences and mental health issues, it made sense to treat these situations as teachable moments for the bully. Perhaps the bully didn't know how to be friends or know how to dislike someone without being physically or verbally abusive. With the patience I had shown my son, he was able to show remarkable patience with others.

During the time period between his abuse and age ten, I had an opportunity to hear a presentation on personal safety. The presenter told the following story. Two friends were camping in the deep woods. They were awakened by the sound of a bear trying to get into their tent. After scooting out the back of the tent, one of the friends noticed the other had grabbed his sneakers and was trying to put them on. The friend asked him what he was doing, as it was likely that he could not outrun the bear anyway. The one with the sneakers responded, "I don't have to outrun the bear; I have to outrun you." Throughout the remainder of the presentation, his point became clear. It is possible to ensure you are the least likely target. By constantly talking with each other, being respectful without taking anything unwanted from others, and conducting ourselves honestly and confidently, we were well on our way to being least likely targets.

We were so intent on making sure that no new abusive situations occurred that we did not plan for the possibility that we would run into one of the former perpetrators. My son was in the first grade at the school where my mother taught. There was a week when my mother was out of town, which necessitated drop-off and pick up to his class directly. He must have seen the female abuser a couple of days before I did, as he had some symptoms of stress such as difficulty sleeping, getting easily frustrated, and difficulty focusing. After dropping him off one of the mornings, I saw her on my way out to the parking lot. She saw me and quickly turned in another direction. By the time I got to my car, my palms were bleeding from where my fingernails had dug into them.

I knew that he was safely in his classroom, so I did not need to go to him. I knew the principal was busy getting the school day started and did not need a hysterical mother on her hands. I decided to go to work and call the principal after gathering my thoughts. The principal was aware of my son's history, so it was not difficult to start the conversation with the fact that we had seen one of the perpetrators. This was the first time I had provided a name to the principal. She agreed to check on some things and make some telephone calls and get back to me. She asked if there was anything she could do to ensure my son's safety, and we agreed to further discuss a safety plan once she had more information.

The principal called me later to let me know that the woman was the mother of one of the students in the school and that this student was supposed to be in the custody of her grandmother. She went on to say that she notified authorities of her presence on school grounds, as she was aware that the student was required to have supervised visitation. The authorities reported that they would follow up on the information provided. The principal had also notified my son's classroom teacher that he was not to be alone under any circumstances. We also worked out a plan to ensure no further contact could take place.

I called his former counselor and set up an appointment for a follow-up visit to ensure that there was no lasting damaging effect from the brief contact. Later that day, I told him that I had seen the perpetrator also and that she had run away from me—a wise decision, we agreed. We talked about our success in dealing with this unexpected thing with dignity and strength. We agreed that it is how we handle the worst things in our lives that define us as much as those things that come easily to us.

There were much larger issues that remained too big for my son to handle. He would ask how to deal with questions of why he was targeted in the first place, how could someone put his own needs ahead of the needs of a child to that extent, or when was he going to stop hurting. There were many questions for which there wasn't a ready "kid's" answer or that required more personal power and experience than he possessed. These, we decided, could not be ignored but needed a safe place to reside until he was ready to deal with them. I proposed we build a "closet in his heart" where these thoughts and questions could be stored.

As his personal power and experience increased, we entered the closet to do some cleaning. Sometimes it was light cleaning, sometimes intense. We discovered the answers to some of the questions and decided to let other thoughts and questions go, as there would be no answers. Sometimes the answers we got raised more questions that took the place of the question we had just cleared. Through it all, whether we emptied part of the closet or not, we did everything we could to strengthen his heart so he could easily bear this burden that only he could carry, full or empty.

There were many times that the pain he carried and the pain I felt on his behalf threatened to crush us. At those times, opportunities to build ourselves up would make themselves known. Numerous interests, activities and contacts with loved ones strengthened our resolve to not become statistics and continue to have fun and laughter. He was safe and could deal with whatever came next from a position of safety.

Self-control came from personal growth and discipline. This is where my experience as a caseworker proved useful. The families with whom I worked taught me through direct example about parenting skills that worked with their children. They also taught me indirectly through examples of parenting that did not work.

Most of my parenting techniques and thoughts on personal power solidified while my son experienced ages six through ten. Looking back, I can identify those that had the most influence. The top seven are as follows:

1) Pick your battles. Many people take this to mean that you must choose what things about which you will fight *against* your children. I take it to mean that there are battles that you must fight *beside* your children. Let's say that your daughter has made it clear that she is going to do all of the things her boyfriend says and not do what you ask. Conventional thinking says to confront her and exert your authority. In this form

of parenting, your next conversation would go something like this:

Mother (calm at first): "I need to talk to you about this boyfriend of yours."

Daughter (wary): "What about him?"

M (serious): "I'm worried that he has too much influence over the decisions you make."

D (becoming defensive): "You don't trust me."

M (becoming defensive): "I trust you. I don't trust him."

D (angry): "It's the same thing since I chose him."

M (angry): "It is not, and don't raise your voice to me."

D (crying): "Don't worry. We don't ever have to talk again."

Another example between a father and son might go like this:

Father (calm at first): "You came home drunk last night."

Son (with a hangover and seeking a hasty end to the conversation): "Yeah."

F (serious): "You know we can't have that. What were you thinking?"

S (becoming defensive): "I wasn't thinking anything."

F (becoming frustrated): "That's obvious."

S (angry): "Then why did you ask?"

F (angry): "You know what? Forget I asked. You're grounded until further notice."

Now imagine how much different things can be if you redefine *battle*. I have never been in the military, but it seems to me that there is probably a pattern to follow for maximum effect. First, you must decide your objective. In both of the above examples, the objective is to have an effective conversation with your child that ensures a change in an unwanted behavior. Next, you must identify your enemy. Herein lies the most important aspect of what I believe and it is this: your child is *never* the enemy. The enemies are peer pressure, over-whelming expectations, isolation, and rejection. Once you have determined your objective and enemy, choose a side (and stay on it). Now imagine how things will go and prepare through mental imaging and practice with someone else. Choose your battlefield and go. In the case of the teenage daughter and boyfriend, invite the boyfriend and see if it can go like this:

M (calm): "I'm glad that you and your boyfriend could take some time to talk today."

D (wary): "Yeah, but we're in a hurry, so could you speed this up."

M (calm): "Sure. I've noticed that when there is some-thing I want you to do that is different than something your boyfriend wants you to do, you end up doing what he wants."

Boyfriend (knowingly): "So?"

D (becoming defensive): "Yeah, so?"

M (calm and to her daughter): "I just wanted you to know that this isn't about what we want you to do. It is about what you want to do. It was never my intention to make you feel like you had to choose between us. You have a great mind of your own, and I have confidence that you will use it. I had been used to you following my advice most of the time and wasn't ready to give that up. I taught you to be loyal to your friends and to be independent. I don't believe you need to reject all of my wishes to accomplish that."

D (becoming calm): "Yeah. That makes sense."

B (unsure): "Can we go now?"

M (calm): "Sure. Please give this some more thought and let me know what you think. I'll see you later. Love you. Bye."

D (relieved): "Love you. Bye."

In the case of the father and son it could go like this:

F (calm and having waited until son is physically ready): "You came home drunk last night."

S (wary): "Yeah."

F (calm): "I've been thinking about all the times that you weren't drunk when you came home and wondering what kind of pressure it took to give in this time."

S (overwhelmed): "I don't know what was different. I was saying no when I got there, but then the next thing I knew, I was drinking."

F (calm): "Let's go through the night step by step. Maybe we can figure out what went wrong and come up with a plan to avoid it next time."

S (thinking): "It won't be easy; I don't remember much."

F (reassuring): "You don't have to remember everything for us to make a plan. Just remember that you have been successful until last night and you can do it again. Do you want to talk about it now or take sometime to think and come back?"

S (reassured): "Let me think about it, and we can talk tonight. I'm guessing I'm not going anywhere."

F (smiling): "Good guess. You won't be going out again until we are both confident you have a plan that will work next time."

In both of the examples, you can see a shift that moves from dead end conversations to open conversations. When your children are little, one conversation is all that is usually needed to resolve an issue. The older they get, the more they need to have brief conversations with a running theme. Leaving the door open for further discussion after everyone has a chance to think things over between conversations is a useful tool. This does not mean there are no consequences for unacceptable behavior. Our children are accountable for their decisions as we are accountable for supporting their battle against poor decisions.

2) Spare the rod; spoil the child. It is widely believed that this means we should strike our children as a means of discipline. I have looked up the meaning of the word *rod* and have discovered two important things. As it relates to the scripture in which the statement is found, the rod refers to a tool used by a shepherd. It is a tool used to guide the sheep away from danger and keep danger away from the sheep. It is not used to strike or beat the sheep.

The other meaning refers to an offshoot or branch of a family tribe. This meaning suggests that separation from connection to family can also result in spoiling a child's future. It is due to this second meaning that I provided my son with access to information about his dad's heritage and encouraged regular contact with his dad's extended family. They thoroughly enjoyed my son's company and shared information about their family histories to ensure connection.

The use of the rod as guide resulted in teaching about respect, integrity, and responsibility. Respect started with basic manners. Use of manners was a way to demonstrate respect toward others. As he got older, communication techniques to avoid arguments and express needs politely were put into place. In preparation for being a teenager, respect as it related to attitude was discussed. With the NVLD, it was imperative that he knew there needed to be a match between his attitude and behaviors also.

Integrity required an understanding of the morals and beliefs that were important to our family. There were *things* that we held in esteem such as an education, a home, and taking care of our possessions. There were *feelings* that we held in esteem such as love, gratitude, and happiness. There were *ideas* that we held in esteem such as peace, kindness, and selflessness. There were *beliefs* that we held in esteem such as faith, hard work, and grace. This was a lot to teach, but all moments for teaching and learning allowed for a lesson in at least one of these. Whether putting toys away, sending a thank-you note, averting an argument, or helping someone pick up something he dropped, we demonstrated what we held in esteem.

Responsibility had many facets. This was a difficult concept for me to grasp as I watched countless families struggle with taking no responsibility whatsoever or, more frequently, taking ineffective responsibility. Consider the family in which a parent demands that his child not strike anyone. The parent emphasizes this point by striking the child. When the child is in school, he strikes other children. When called in to the school, the parent defends the child. Confusion, chaos, and continued physical aggression were always the result.

It took some time for me to see this as a responsibility issue. I wanted my discipline to reflect that I was responsible *for* teaching about right from wrong. I was also responsible *for* demonstrating good choices. Once my son learned what was right, he became responsible *for* choosing to do what was right. I then became responsible *to* ensure he did so. This took the form of reminders, practice, and consequences if necessary. If a thing is wrong to do, it is wrong no matter who is doing it.

Responsibility is not just about behaviors. It is also about feelings. While trying to help my son recognize my facial expressions when I was feeling something, I learned the importance of owning responsibility for the feeling. This became a great benefit to me, as expressing and describing my feelings brought me to an honest relationship with my son.

The term *losing it* was often used to describe someone

becoming enraged or out of control. It begged the questions: "What is *it*?" and "If I'm *losing it*, who has *it*?" If *it* is my feelings, then I don't want someone else to bear them, especially if *someone else* is my eight-year-old son. If *it* is my control, then I don't want to give that to someone else, especially if *someone else* is my eight-year-old son.

My feelings belong to me. It is my responsibility to effectively deal with unwanted feelings without giving them to someone else. An example would be coming home from a difficult day at work. Tired and frustrated, I yell at my young son for forgetting to put his book bag away. Now, he is frustrated and, because the frustration didn't belong to him in the first place, begins to seek a way of getting rid of it. I have watched the members of families give frustration and anger back and forth to each other for years on end.

A child will do the same with unwanted feelings. It seemed as if doing this was the easiest and most likely thing to do when upset or angry. Once again we needed to get specific and diligent about what needed to change and in so doing, it is now automatic for us to try not to give our feelings to others and not accept the unwanted feelings others try to give to us.

In practice it sounds like this:

Son (while throwing his math book across the room): "This is stupid, and you can't make me do it."

Mother (while trying not to get angry in response): "This math is harder than you thought; pick up the book, and let's take a look at it together."

S (while picking up his math book and still frustrated): "What if you don't know how to do it either?"

M (with a small smile): "I can see that you are angry and frustrated, but let's let today be the last day that you can't do this math, even if I have to call for help too."

The fact is if we get angry *with* the child, nothing gets done. If we get angry *instead* of the child, nothing gets done. If we get angry *because* of the child, nothing gets done. Address the anger effectively first. Once the unwanted feeling is gone, things can get done.

The definitions for the *rod* as guidance and connection with family are most useful in helping to determine effective discipline and corrective methods with all children. Some people learn with humor, some with smallest step directions, and some with visual reminders. Just like all those times that you tried to get your baby to eat something new by gagging down a spoonful yourself, use yourself as the best guide and source of connection for your unspoiled child.

3) Closure. There is no such thing! I am probably not the only person tired of hearing the word. It is meant to suggest that there can be an end to unwanted feelings of grief, isolation, or financial issues (to name but a few) because of an outside force, waiting for someone or something else to occur that will determine whether we carry unwanted feelings breeds mistrust, ingratitude, and hopelessness.

It has become natural for us to decide that we will feel better as long as the thing we want has happened. I will feel better when I have a new house, the abuser of my child is punished, or I get the perfect job. When this doesn't happen, we tend to blame others for not doing their part. This blame can be levied against family members, a boss, even friends. Trust in others as well as ourselves reduces over time.

For many of us, the thing we want will never happen. We are so busy being miserable while waiting for the thing we want, we miss being grateful for having the things we have. When others get something they want or don't lose what we have lost, we cannot even celebrate with them. Statements such as "That's nice, but..." begin to permeate our conversations as nothing seems able to satisfy.

When we feel we have waited too long for something we want, we give up. It becomes pointless to ask for anything. Praying for others doesn't even bring the promise it once did. A general feeling that nothing can make a difference enters into our attitude, our decision making, and our relationships.

Imagine being a child in a home where mistrust, ingratitude, and hopelessness prevail. There is nothing he can do to prove his love, as any attempts to do so are met with distrust. There is no way to gain approval for a job well done or even be told thank you. The message of *give up* can be impossible to overcome.

I propose that if we can decide that we will feel better after some outside force occurs, then we can decide to feel better while we are waiting! I don't want someone or something else to decide if I am going to be happy or not. It is not my intention to minimize the effect that great loss, illness, or abuse can have on an individual or a family. It is only my intention to suggest that those things do not have to define us or determine the path our lives will take.

4) Personal power. Things were different when we were younger in many ways. I remember when people in our communities cared whether the children were making safe decisions or not. When we went outside to play and an adult saw us do something we shouldn't, he or she would yell at us and then call our parents so we would get yelled at when we got home. The same was true if anyone tried to hurt us or we were hurt while playing. Adults in our communities would protect us and then let our parents know. This is no longer the case. In

fact, not only do other adults fail to intervene when children get into trouble, they get a hostile response from the parent if they try.

Our children are now responsible for their safety whenever they leave our homes. As such, they must be armed with all of the things we can give them in order to succeed. I used this analogy of "armor" with my son, and we broke it down into the components of armor such as shield, helmet, and various parts of the suit itself.

Information about obvious and hidden dangers was the shield. This included keeping a safe distance from strangers (defined as anyone whose home we haven't entered). It also included an understanding that people who wish to cause harm often appear to be kind at first. He knew better than anyone that someone trusted could cause serious harm.

The shield is also meant to protect the vital organs, especially the heart, from attack. Making sure that he was protected physically was necessary when he could not protect himself. As he got older and more able to protect himself physically, the shield became necessary as difficulties in various relationships threatened to break his heart. Arguments with his dad, friends that betrayed him in some way, and breaking up with girlfriends required their own special shield. In these cases, the protection came from the belief that nothing could permanently end his relationship with his dad, he deserved to have friends that treated him with respect, and that even the pain of a breakup subsides.

The helmet was knowledge. The more information he had about a situation, the more successful he was at navigating it. The same is true for all children. It is what they don't know that gets them into trouble. The first time they are old enough to realize their parents have left them with someone else, they do not know their parents will return. The first time they go to school, they don't know all the rules. The first time they are faced with a difficult choice to which they do not have a practiced response, they cannot see all of the possible consequences.

Every time that Ben needed more information, I would provide it. I usually started those conversations with the words "here's the thing…" (He became so accustomed to me doing so that he would always add, "Because there is always a thing.") Perhaps he is right. There is always one more thing to learn, one more thing to teach, and one more thing that can make life easier to understand and navigate.

The other pieces of the armor are to protect from lesser issues. Being called names, losing a favorite toy, and failing a test are a few of the lesser issues. If these things happen often enough, they too can threaten a child's sense of personal power. These are easily protected through hearing as many positive statements about themselves at home as possible, teaching them to take care of their things, and providing assistance to be successful in school.

It isn't always outside forces that threaten our children's personal power. Sometimes the negative forces are within. Nagging thoughts of doubt, pessimism, and worthlessness conspire to immobilize our children. This results in isolation, the need to strike first, and put others down in an attempt to make themselves feel better.

These negative forces can have many sources, such as an unresolved mental health issue, unresolved trauma, or an environment in which the child is taught he is worthless and nothing good will come of his existence. Whatever the source, the treatment is the same. Anyone with such overwhelming negative thoughts needs to get them out in the open where they can be confronted and replaced with positive thoughts. With encouragement, repeated opportunities for experiences to have a positive outcome, and believing that everyone has worth, even these overwhelming negative forces from within are something against which our children can be protected.

5) Boundaries/Transparency. At first glance, these terms may seem to be contradictory. For most of us, the word *boundaries* carries the connotation that we need to keep some type of separation between our selves and others. We do so at work when we do not want to mix what happens at home with what we are expected to produce. We do so at church when we believe that the needs of others are greater than our own. We do so with our children when we need to protect them from harsh realities for which they are not ready.

Boundaries are also the means by which we decide how we will live with one another. They are comprised of the rules and expectations we have. These rules are based on the behaviors we will tolerate (acceptable) and those we will not (unacceptable). We even have rules for how we will negotiate behaviors that fall in the in-between stages. For example, I will tolerate any assistance from my son in taking care of the house. I will not tolerate any willful destruction of property. I will negotiate what my response will be if something breaks as the result of an accident.

Ben had so many questions about what was acceptable and how he could tell. When I was a child, I do not remember asking as many questions. I remember that when I did, answers were provided for the most part. Mostly, I tried to figure out what confused me on my own. Ben and I had learned that he would not necessarily figure things out on his own. If you have a child in your home that does not figure things out so easily, then explanations are needed to maintain boundaries. You may have a child for whom the things that a child needs to know came easily but has difficulty figuring out how to be a teenager in your home.

It should be noted that most things fall in that in-between behavior stage. It is the constant negotiation with our children of what is acceptable and unacceptable that exhausts us. When my son was around age six we were playing a game of chess. When the telephone rang, I got up to answer it. The call took longer than expected, and when my son interrupted me to ask a question, I pointed out his mistake and asked him to wait. He waited patiently from there but sat watching me closely. When the telephone call ended, he asked me if I had pointed out to the caller his mistake in interrupting us in the first place. We agreed that I would offer him the common courtesy of asking him to excuse me when I answered the telephone after that.

We take for granted that the skills of the child will translate when he becomes a teenager. Even the simplest rule to not take something that does not belong to you is different when you need to take your best friend's car keys to keep him from driving drunk. As the rules change, as more reasoning is necessary to make the right choices, and as they experience more pressure to do the wrong things, our children need transparency from us.

Transparency provides our children with the information they need in order to make decisions without us when the time comes. Clarity regarding our desired outcome for their lives as well as how to make good decisions will be of great use to our children as they get older. I remember when I was a child and all of my friends thought I was a spoiled brat. The reason they thought this was that I always seemed to get my way. What they did not know was that I got my way so often because I did not waste my time asking for anything to which I knew my parents would say no.

My parents' transparency with me was as follows: no meant no; safety was most important; supervision was necessary for that safety; all information was needed to make an affirmative decision; and some things cost too much. Every good parent out there knows that when a child asks for permission for something, at least twenty questions come immediately to mind.

Let's take for example the question, "Can I go to my friend's house?" Before the question is even finished, we want to know: what friend; who else will be there; will there be an adult; how are you going to get there; how will you get back; did you have any problems the last time you went; if so, have they been resolved; how long do you plan to be there; have you finished your chores; is your homework done; do their parents know you are coming; you always go there, isn't it our turn to have him here; what will you do once you are there; if you decide to go somewhere else, how will you let me know…

The list goes on and on depending on past experiences and how well known the friend is to you. These questions need to be asked out loud. When our children know what information we need in order to be able to say yes to an activity, it makes for much shorter conversations and far more yes answers. Once I had trained Ben with the information I was going to need, I didn't have to ask any questions when he asked to go out. He would simply come to me and say, "Mom, I would like to go to Jeremiah's house. We are going to practice playing our guitars and talk to some friends online. It's early enough for me to walk there, but later we want to come back here for dinner and have him stay overnight; we will need a ride. His mom will be there until we are ready to come back here." Jeremiah was his best friend, so I already had telephone numbers and knew his mother. Whatever information Ben knew that I didn't have, he would supply in his request.

I have watched most parents struggle with these conversations as their children became more and more frustrated with questions they were not prepared to answer because they were not taught how to ask if they could go out. And then as the parents received an answer of "I don't know" to every question, they would become frustrated and just say no to make the agony end.

Our children can be provided with the basic information that we will need whenever they ask permission for something. If the request requires more specific information and conditions in order for you to say yes, then say so in a way they can understand. Asking to go to a friend's house carries the usual questions. Asking if you can go to a concert has some special questions.

When my son wanted to go to Woodstock 1999, I provided a list of conditions that would make me feel safe saying yes. These conditions were also exceptionally difficult to meet. They were that he would find an adult to take him that I trusted completely, that this adult would be able to accompany him to every aspect of the concert (including the bathroom), and that the adult would have the authority to tell him to do something and he would do it immediately.

It turns out that I had taught my son very well, not just about how to make sure that I could say yes to a request, but also in being able to figure out the best person to ask to take him. He started with people nearby, such as his godfather and his godparent's adult sons. When they said no, he carefully listened to their reasons of being too old, not wanting to take the responsibility, not being interested in the music, and not having the money or transportation. When Ben overheard a conversation I was having with my brother about him having laser surgery so he wouldn't have to wear glasses, coloring his hair, and maybe getting a tattoo, Ben asked if he could speak to his uncle. The two of them had a very good time at Woodstock.

Getting all the answers you need in order to say yes to a request does not mean that you will say yes. Sometimes we need to say no because we have information our child does not. When this happens, it is also necessary to be as transparent as we can. There was a time when I did not want him walking to his best friend's home because of an increase in gang violence between our two homes, so the rule about saying yes to walking over there changed. When he wanted to go see his bass guitar teacher play a couple of sets at a bar that was having an alcohol-free night for teenagers, I said no without being able to give an explanation. The next day on the news, there was a story about a fight and stabbing that took place outside that bar during the event.

The authority to say yes or no to the requests of our children remain with the parent. It is with the use of boundaries and transparency that we make decisions with, and on behalf of, our children. As difficult as this process may be at times, it is easier than trying to undo wrong choices after the fact.

6) Half-full/Half-empty. Before I knew that Ben would suffer from Generalized Anxiety Disorder, I thought that optimism was preferable to pessimism. Take the illustration of the glass that is half filled with water. To me, it is not half empty. It is not half full either. It is full—half is water and the other half is air. This level of optimism sometimes threatened to drive my son crazy, but it would end up being a good balance for him later in life.

From age six to eleven, we worked on the things that I would say or do that impacted negatively on how he viewed the world. There are three that stand out the most when I think back on that time. The first was asking questions to which I already knew the answer. I don't know why parents do this. Maybe we hope they will redeem themselves by being truthful. Maybe we want to catch them lying. Maybe it happened to us so we do it. Whatever the reason, we usually end up compounding a bad situation.

One of the questions we ask to which we usually know the answer is "Did you do this?" If the child says he didn't do it, the behavior we wanted to correct in the first place gets lost when we argue over whether the child did it or not. If he is prepared to say he did it, he becomes mistrustful of our motives when we ask a question. When we know of a certainty that our child has done something wrong, then name it and make a decision on the consequence.

Another mistake I made was reacting too quickly. Unless a child is about to stick his hand on a hot stove (or something else dangerous) we have time to decide how we are going to respond. Taking time allows us to see things all the way through. This includes how our actions may effect how our children see us as well as the world. Have you ever looked at yourself in the mirror while you were screaming? Give it a try. I'll bet you stop and turn away. Yet we expect our children to face us when we are yelling and haven't taken the time to calm down first.

My third largest mistake was using the word *but*. The bed you made looks good, *but* it is still sloppy. Thank you for taking out the garbage, *but* you should have done it last night. I love you, *but* you get on my last nerve. We spoke of some issues that have a negative impact on how our children view us and the world. What does this say about how they will view themselves? Over time, they will expect every compliment to come with criticism. How can anyone stay positive or optimistic in the face of that?

Just by switching to the word *and*, I was able to change my use of the word *but*. When I told Ben he had done a good job on something, I could add a suggestion with the word *and* instead of a criticism. That small shift allowed for much more positive communication and forced me to pay attention to what was being said. Paying attention leads to carefulness. Carefulness leads to encouragement. Encouragement leads to success. Success leads to optimism!

7) This isn't about me. This is one of the most important things to remember. So much of what was written in the first six principles is based on this concept. In the extremes, there are two reasons to have children. The first is that the person or couple has their own needs fulfilled and wish to provide life and love to a new human being. The other extreme is that the person or couple wishes to fulfill their own needs.

In the case of the first, the parents are prepared for how needy an infant is. They know that there will be sleepless nights, fun activities missed, and sacrifices to make. The needs of the child come first. Selfless is the best way to describe these parents. There may be some complaints along the way, but for the most part they cannot wait to see their friends to talk about their child's activities, abilities, and accomplishments. By their example, they teach their children to put the needs of others ahead of their own. Though it is not sought, their children even put their parents' needs ahead of their own at times.

In the case of the second, the parents are unprepared to meet the needs of the infant. Instead of filling the emptiness, they feel the child comes into the world demanding and represents the epitome of self-absorption. These parents have nothing but complaints and find their child capable of doing nothing right. No matter how hard this child tries to meet the needs this type of parent has, he will fail. In failing, he becomes inconsolably depressed or irreconcilably defiant.

Most of us fall somewhere in between these extremes and can even fall in different places on the spectrum depending on current life circumstances. The reality is that none of us is perfect, and there are a number of events that impact our ability to respond in a healthy way to our children. When we keep in mind that the actions, needs, and decisions of our children are not about us, we are far more likely to respond well.

Take for example the child that has accidentally spilled something in a restaurant. The selfless parent sees this as a natural function of the growing child. She is prepared to ask for extra napkins (which she usually already has in anticipation of such an occurrence) and assists the child with cleanup. Jokes about spilling follow, and everyone is put at ease with the event.

The selfish parent sees this as an embarrassment and seeks to embarrass the child in return with yelling and negative comments. An attempt is made to gain sympathy and understanding from the people nearby with rolled eyes, heavy sighs, and comments that others are expected to overhear. This just makes anyone nearby uncomfortable, causes the child unnecessary embarrassment, and does nothing to make the parent look better.

For the most part, I remembered that my child came first. There were times when I was selfish and felt the sting of it later, wishing I hadn't said certain things or when remembering the look on my child's face when I did something that was designed to make me (and only me) feel better. As I said to myself over and over again, "This isn't about me," I began to change how I saw my relationship with Ben and thereby put his needs in his context.

While I knew that we decided to have a child because of what we had to give, there were some things that took an effort to accept gracefully. When my son was little and it took two hours to describe an event that lasted one hour("…and then…you know what…and then…"), I somehow found the respect to listen. When he was a teenager and it took one word to describe an event that lasted four hours ("fine"), I somehow found the patience to wait for him to tell me more. When his loyalty to his friends sometimes threatened to draw him into the difficulties they were having, I somehow found the courage to trust. When he said "I hate you" in a fit of rage, I somehow found the strength to love.

Say it to yourself every time you face something in your child that threatens to make you think of yourself first. Say it to yourself every time you must give up something that you enjoy to meet the needs of your child. Say it to yourself every time the first thought in your head begins with the word *I*. Please feel free to say it out loud if saying it in your head is not enough. Try it on for size. "This isn't about me."

Reinstating trust was also necessary for us to move past the experience of abuse Ben had suffered. As with everything else in our lives, I had to learn it first, like all of the other things I had learned before my son was born. Everything that he needed to learn, I had to relearn first.

I often spoke to my mother about the doubts, fears, and feelings of rage that I had about what had happened to Ben. She listened to everything that had been happening to me with the utmost patience. That is until she could no longer stand to see me in such obvious pain and blurted out, "How can you say the Lord's Prayer with any meaning? Especially the section on forgiving?"

She needed me to understand the power of forgiveness. She needed me to understand that in the absence of forgiveness, the abusers had the power to decide how I felt. If the abusers knew how miserable I was, wouldn't that make them happy? She also wanted me to know what my lack of forgiveness was doing to my son and my relationship with the Father.

I was, and am, overwhelmed and humbled by how much I have to learn. I had addressed the power that the perpetrators had *taken* away but had failed to see the power I had *given* away. What a relief to finally let it go. I still cannot say the Lord's Prayer without feeling tears when saying the words "forgive us our trespasses as we forgive those who trespass against us." Jesus did not tell us to say this because we wouldn't be forgiven if we didn't forgive others. He told us to do so because He knew how much He had to forgive and the power that comes with it. There are no words to describe the feeling that happens when you honestly forgive someone else. Power does not cover it. Peace does not cover it. Free does not cover it. Perhaps a word that means all three can come close.

Forgiving allowed me to learn how to trust again. This trust had to be extended toward the Father in the form of understanding that He was hurting as much as I was that this kind of suffering occurs. Trust had to be extended to myself in the form of understanding that I can provide protection and avoid opportunities for abuse. Trust had to be extended to others in the form of understanding that Ben had already come into contact with a large number of people for whom abusing him never entered their minds.

No longer encumbered by unresolved issues with my son's abuse, I was able to give him the strength to grow in many ways. No longer grieving over the loss of the relationship with his father, I was able to encourage Ben to love his father without reservation. No longer unsure of how my son learned new things, I was able to teach him how he learned so he could do more for himself.

I could only watch in awe as he grew during this time period from age six to eleven. Both adults and children listened to him. People in restaurants offered him money, reporting that they had been moved by how well behaved he was. I received notes from his dad's extended family telling me what a joy he is. During a visit with his dad's parents, he had a conversation with a physicist regarding the question, which is more intelligent, the universe or a human. He listened quietly for some time to both sides of the argument. When he was asked what he thought, he responded that a human is more intelligent because a human has the ability to ask the question. He was six years old.

He appeared to be at ease. He learned how to ride a bike, made new friends, and learned right from wrong. He found music. Someone introduced him to the trumpet and in so doing opened a world for him that would have far reaching effects. We attended the United Methodist Church regularly, and he chose to be baptized when he was seven.

By the time he was eleven years old, nothing could shake him. Ben carried himself with dignity and poise. He found joy in the simplest of things and could make an entire room full of people stop in their tracks, whether to laugh at something he said or at some incredible insight with the turn of a phrase. He read everything, played trumpet and chess, and brought a smile to the face of all who saw him. How could anything stop him now? Through it all, my prayer remained, "This child belongs to the Father."

Crash

Seventh grade. Within days of turning twelve, it happened. With the force of a sixty-mile-per-hour car crash, Ben was stopped dead in his tracks by his first Generalized Anxiety Disordered attack and first psychotic break.

I received a telephone call from his dad's resident girl-friend. She had received a call from Ben's school letting her know that he had been found sitting on the floor of the boys' bathroom, rocking himself, and saying over and over again, "They finally killed my mother." While rushing to her home to get him, there were so many things going through my mind. Maybe someone that he trusted had told him that I had been killed. Maybe he had seen a news program and thought the victim looked like me. Maybe they had called the wrong parent and it was happening to someone else.

When I arrived, he was inconsolable, and he didn't even believe I was alive when I was standing right in front of him. Slowly, he came back to reality, and we went home. We called the specialized Kid's Help Line at our local crisis services so he could talk. The next day, we scheduled to go see the counselor he always saw and this time added a psychiatrist appointment.

By this time in his life, I had fifteen years of experience working in the mental health field with children and was well on my way to securing a master's degree in counseling psychology. When it happens to your own child, there is no such thing as prepared. I turned to professionals to assist us in getting through this process. While the skills I had learned as a professional would help me to identify when the services we received were of benefit, there was no way that I could provide the professional assistance that he needed when both of us were hurting.

He refused to return to school at first. My mother was retired, so she went with him for a short period of time while we started counseling in the hopes that it would help enough to get him to be less anxious about school. I did not want to add any phobias to his growing list of obstacles to overcome, so giving up school was out of the question. When it was clear that a week of my mother going to school with him was not going to be long enough, I took an unpaid leave of absence from work under the Family Medical Leave Act in order to ensure he felt safe enough to continue.

When I first proposed it to the assistant principal, he was not in favor of the idea. It was acceptable for my mother, a retired teacher from the same school district, to be there for what was expected to be short a period of time. Allowing me to be in the school for what appeared to be an indefinite amount of time was not as easy for him to accept.

Their first response was to recommend an evaluation by the Committee on Special Education and from there, a more appropriate educational placement. I politely explained that Ben did not meet the criteria for such a recommendation, let alone the criteria for a different educational placement. I further explained that it would cost the district no extra money to allow me to try something different to avoid such a costly placement. I also promised them that I was capable of causing great upset within the district if they failed to provide me the opportunity to intervene on my son's behalf.

For the first week, I sat in the back of each of his classes so that he could turn to see me for reassurance. Each day that passed without an anxiety attack was celebrated. When attacks happened anyway, we dealt with them and immediately returned to schoolwork. For the remaining weeks of my leave, I was stationed in the office or the library for easy access.

As his need to find me reduced, we began to discuss the next step. This step was for me to return to work but be in the office for the hours that he was in school so he could call me if needed. After two months, I was able to return to my usual workday, which required being in the field and not always having immediate access. My mother was on call for emergencies, but by then we didn't need it.

This does not mean that there were not times of intense anxiety, frustration, and sadness. We had assigned a rating system to how he experienced his anxiety, and he was determined to use every coping skill he had in order to maintain control. Accepting that he did not have control over whether or not he had anxiety and to what degree did not mean that he couldn't find a way to cope effectively. He called the Kid's Help Line at crisis services almost every night. I called crisis services every night after he went to bed to do my own crying and talking things through. We slowly came to not need them, but we will never forget their assistance during that time.

He was going to counseling and had seen the psychiatrist for the first time. The psychiatrist explained Generalized Anxiety Disorder and recommended an antidepressant medication. Ben nodded his head in understanding, I accepted the prescription, and we went to the car. Once in the car, Ben began to sob. I waited until he could speak; making him speak before he was ready with constant questions only made him more anxious. When he could speak, he stated that he thought he "could take care of it himself." I told him that taking the medication was how he was going to take care of it himself. I also told him that I didn't understand how it came to be that people have no problem getting a cast and medication for pain when they have a broken arm but will not get counseling (cast) and medication for their pain when they have something "broken" in their head. I told him that we were not going to make that mistake, and he had every right to accept everything that could make it better.

There were things that our professionals didn't tell us. They were things that I knew, and so I did not think about it at the time. Let me take a few moments here to explain why I was all right with medication for my son. I know that there has been a lot of discussion lately about antidepressants increasing the risk of suicide in adolescents and young adults. In all of that discussion, I did not once hear anyone explain what counselors have known for decades and it is this: when people start to feel better after a deep depression or anxiety, they will consider suicide as a means to make sure they never feel that badly again.

Antidepressant medications result in a person feeling better. Feeling better or stronger is also necessary in order for someone to carry out his or her thoughts of suicide. Add to it that most children and young adults do not have a future focus and you have the combination necessary for increased risk. Increased risk does not mean suicide. It does mean that professionals need to tell their clients the warning signs to look for and interventions necessary to avert attempts. It is not the failure of the medication to bring relief to the pain; it is the failure of the "cast" to hold things in place until the healing has taken place. The cast is made up of counselors, family, educators, faith, trust, and personal resolve. All must work together for success.

There were so many things that surprised me during this time period. One of the biggest was how he was received at the school by his peers when I was there. You would think that they only treated him nicely when I was there or because I was there. Instead, they were very generous and solicitous toward him whether I was there or not. They quickly became used to my presence and would let the teacher know if Ben needed me and could not speak. This is not the way junior high school students usually react to one another, and it was another reason to be grateful.

Another surprise was how easy it was to stop doing all of the things that he had done before in favor of trying to be still in the hopes that stillness would keep anxiety attacks from coming. Among the things that were put aside were the trumpet, chess, swimming, and going to friends' houses. He turned all of his attention to movies and books. He wanted to be a director, and this seemed another way to exercise some control over his surroundings.

His stuttering intensified. His avoidance of anything new happened daily. His self-confidence diminished. His coping skills were stretched to the breaking point and beyond. Laughter, poise, and self-esteem were slowly disappearing. We were in trouble, and it didn't help that our beliefs could not stop what was happening. How many times can you continue to believe that everything will be all right in the face of the painful realities in front of you?

When our church decided to close, we decided to stop going to any church. It wasn't a conscious decision, but I think that on some level we thought we couldn't make things worse by trying to do for ourselves. We had always put our faith and trust in the Father and look how good things were turning out.

This is when we learned that a brain divided against itself cannot stand any more than a country can. Ben's brain was in constant turmoil. His brain was never fully relaxed, as it anticipated that another anxiety attack could come at any moment. His entire being reflected the conflict within. He cried often, slept little, and jumped at every move. When he experienced an anxiety attack, the event preceding it was examined intensely to determine if it could and/or should be avoided. I allowed for a certain amount of avoidance because it became easier than running the risk of triggering an attack that would further solidify the faulty belief that there were identifiable causes for his anxiety.

The medication finally started to take the edge off of his anxiety and reduce the number of attacks. Discussions could finally take place when there was no anxiety that could be used to strengthen and increase his coping skills. These took on the usual format. Information and being able to use words to explain what was happening began to take shape. This started with explaining why his brain insisted I was dead during that first psychotic break. The explanation was that he knew he was hurting in a way he had never hurt before and his brain sought an explanation. My death was the only thing possible that could explain the amount of pain he was in. His brain already had a way to explain it when it combined this belief with the memory of the perpetrators saying they would kill me if he told what they were doing to him.

We learned that it was all right to cry for no apparent reason. We learned that anxiety attacks would pass as mysteriously as they had begun and to attach any more significance to it than the fleeting pain of a stubbed toe was to our disadvantage. We learned that there was no way to predict them, completely stop them, or make them end more quickly once they

Wendy Morse

had begun. For better or worse, they were what they were. When weeks began to go by without one, we did not miss them, but we also did not despair if one came. Ben has Generalized Anxiety Disorder, and no amount of time between attacks would mean that it was over.

Slowly, remarkably, the jokes returned. When going to a funny movie with friends, he would comment that this would not be a good time for an anxiety attack. When participating in a particularly solemn occasion and having trouble mustering the appropriate sad response, he would comment that it was a good time for an anxiety attack. The first time that he had a group of friends over to spend the night after he had started on his medications, everyone burst out laughing when I handed Ben his morning medication, which prompted two of his friends to remember they had medications for migraines and ADHD to take. When he had been worried that no one would understand that he needed them, it turned out that his friends did understand.

Once again, we found our balance. The counseling worked. The medication did its part. Life began to return to what it had been. Ben's primary interest continued to be movie directing. He also began to be interested in new kinds of music.

Most importantly, he began to do something for which I was totally unprepared. He started to let me know that he was not always going to do things my way. Most of my friends and family will remember this time as the note time. After repeating myself a number of times on a particular issue, I decided to put a note up where it could be read. The notes were for the usual things like turn the light off, use a napkin, and put an empty garbage bag in the bin after you have removed the full one.

There was the time when he shared a handwritten essay that he had done for English class. I read and enjoyed the essay and then asked when it was due. He replied that he was turning it in early. When I suggested that he use the extra time to rewrite it so there would not be anything crossed off, he rolled his eyes. I had completely underestimated the effect this could have on me.

I could barely speak above a whisper as I told him he needed to leave the room before I killed him. Knowing that I was not one for idle threats, he complied immediately. After a time, he returned to the living room and carefully looked inside. By then I was calm enough to explain that I did not know that a simple thing like rolling his eyes would result in such a reaction from me. I went on to say that he had obviously reached an age where he needed to try things for himself. It was important for him to know that he can tell me by reminding me that he was carrying a 98 percent average in English and knew that his teacher would be all right with it. He could have let me know that he wanted to see what would happen if he handed in something that wasn't perfect. He could have let me know that he was tired of the project and didn't much care if he got a slightly lower grade than usual.

In short, I wanted him to know that he can speak to me to let me know that he is getting old enough to make some of his own decisions even if they are different than mine. He also needed to hear me say that being disrespectful to me was never going to be the way to let me know. There would, of course, be a few more incidents of not following my expectations or directions, but this set the stage for a very honest communication between us that would require dialogue to settle difficulties no matter how big.

Wendy Morse

He entered eighth grade prepared with his coping skills. These skills would include finding the teachers that he could trust to assist when needed, being able to contact me when needed, and being able to contact my parents if unable to reach me. He was to be in the same school with the same students that had been so supportive the year before, so we thought we were ready for anything.

This age proved to be more difficult for all of Ben's friends from the previous year. He was being picked on now more than ever. There were fewer symptoms of the anxiety to overcome but far more issues with peers.

I turned to the staff for assistance and again received the initial no response. There are some things for which I will take a no answer. This was not any of them. How quickly they had forgotten my tenacity and resolve. I told the administration that they had the authority to decide if they should ask teachers to be more watchful or provide extra assistance, but they would not stand in my way if I did so. There were teachers that decided to be of more assistance when asked. They became the people Ben would go to whenever there was a problem. Teachers that were not interested in helping probably would not have done so even if the administration asked.

Those that were helpful did more than help as they demonstrated the characteristics and abilities that Ben would later imitate. They were able to have a sense of humor about negative situations, they carried themselves with assurance, and they reminded him of his past poise and confidence.

Ben came home one day from school and reported that I might be getting a call from the assistant principal because of an incident that had happened in the pool. He explained that three of his classmates had cornered him in the shallow end and started calling him names and hitting him. His first thought had been the question I always asked him in situations like this, which was "Where was the teacher?" For the first time, it occurred to him that if the teacher wasn't there to see what these three kids were doing, he was not there to see Ben's reaction. One of them went home with a black eye; the others stopped immediately when he fought back. I told him I was behind him on this.

It is not that I advocate violence in response to violence. It is that I advocate an end to violence. This was the beginning of the end of the violence against him. He told me that he had decided to ask the science teacher to help him talk to these boys one at a time the next day. He did not want the science teacher to tell them what to do, only allow him the opportunity to have a conversation with these three once and for all about how he expected to be treated from then on. The next day, his science teacher invited the boys to speak with Ben separately. It was agreed that there would be no further difficulties among them. The remainder of the school year went blissfully well.

There were discussions about the need for medication with his psychiatrist. When he was functioning well, it was inevitable that someone would ask if he needed to continue to take the medication. At one point, it was decided that he would stop taking the medication to see how things would go. The reaction was obvious, and the medication was reinstated.

At one time, it seemed the medication was not working as well as it had at first, and so it was doubled. At the doubled rate, he had difficulty focusing and completing tasks. The psychiatrist recommended a different medication. It made no sense to me as there was evidence that this medication was the right one. I demanded they try something between the twenty-five milligrams and fifty milligrams. We settled on thirty-seven and a half milligrams, and this would prove to be the right dose for most of the time until he no longer needed it.

Many people with this potentially debilitating disorder continue to struggle with being able to do the simplest of things. I do not mean to minimize their struggle by making this seem like it was easy, because it was not. There were days when we were immobilized. There were times when it seemed impossible for his small body to produce enough fluid for the amount of tears he shed. There were times when I thought his breath would never return to normal as he struggled with the negative thoughts that threatened his very existence.

We talked all of the time. We gave power to the words in his head that could shout down the negative thoughts that appeared. We rated the anxiety he was feeling and came up with a list of matching coping experiences to use when the attacks came. We found the supports necessary to balance his life in a positive direction. We let go of what couldn't be changed. We gave ourselves permission to fall apart when we needed and be strong when we needed. We made it and prepared to face what came next.

He was accepted into the high school he wanted. He went to Woodstock 1999, which took him about as far outside of his comfort zone as any activity could. He carried himself like all of the men he admired. He stood at the top of the next mountain he had climbed and believed he was ready for the next one.

I let myself get used to the idea that he was becoming his own person. I found out that I could not protect him from many things, but the sun still rose and good things still happened. I experienced continued pride and marveled at his resilience. I knew, even in the midst of my separation from things religious, that "this preteen belonged to the Father."

Not the Best Spiritual Leader

Not more than four feet ten inches in his sneakers. Still with red hair and red freckles. The slightest apprehension marked by an increase in his stutter. The first day of high school. Everyone else seemed to tower over him. He belonged there. He was expected there. He was there.

What would this day hold? What would this week hold? What would this year hold? I prayed as usual and continued to miss the irony that I was not making sure that my son continued his relationship with the Father. I had any number of excuses. I worked long hours and was tired by Sunday. I didn't want to force him because that would make him hate religion. I had gone to a couple of churches in the city, and they had small attendance, leading me to the concern that I did not want to be in the congregation of another church that had to close.

Many churches did close in Buffalo, New York, during the years that Ben was in high school. What few remained often had my clients in attendance, which gave me another excuse to stay away. It was selfish of me. I had been raised with all of the old traditions, choir, youth group, and favorite hymns. I deprived him of these and the sense of belonging that they had always engendered in me. I thought I knew everything that would be needed for us to have a good life and did not think that I needed religion to achieve the goals we had set. As long as I prayed and praised the Father in my own way, why did I need to attend church?

As Ben began to exert even more independence in our home, I was content in exerting my independence with the Father. The story "Footprints" was not on my mind, but it was my story. My mother purchased the largest print of the story and gave it to me. I didn't know then what she trying to tell me. I praise the Father that I do now.

Ben walked up the stairs of his new school and entered with confidence. At the end of the day, I rushed to get home to find out how it went. He had large scrapes in the palms of both hands. He explained that he would not get his locker assignment until the end of the first week, which meant that he would need to bring all of his books and supplies to and from school for a time. On his way home, he had tripped and probably would have been able to stay upright had it not been for the hundred pounds of books in his backpack.

This raised an entirely new issue. I had been allowed to get his locks for his lockers in previous years and had always gotten the kind that opened with a key. The dreaded combination lock was just a few days away.

Have you ever had to teach someone that has a sequential learning difference how to open a combination locker? We went out to get one on which to practice. He looked at me like I had lost my mind when I started to explain how they work. I showed him twice and then gave him the lock. For the first number, turn it to the right and pass the number at least three times before you stop on it. Then turn the dial to the left and pass the number only once before stopping on it. Finally, turn the dial to right and stop at the number the first time you come to it.

He practiced until he became quite proud when he opened it several times in a row before announcing that he had mastered the skill. I said he had not and went on to explain that all combination locks had different sets of numbers. He said he understood the need for this, but it did not stop him from hitting his head on the table in anguish.

By morning, he announced that he had a plan and asked me if he could put it into practice before he told me. I said that would be fine. At the end of the first day that he had been given his locker and combination, he shared the plan. He had drawn a map of the school on which he had indicated the location of his classes in reference to the location of the locker. He had then written in the times that it would be most convenient to stop at the locker, taking into account times that he would be passing it on the way to the next class. He found three opportunities to stop at his locker.

He took this map to the school janitor, whom he had discovered had the ability to open all of the lockers with a special key. He had him make a copy for himself and asked if the janitor could be in the vicinity of his locker at the times indicated in case he could not open it right away. It was brilliant, and it worked. By the end of the first week, he no longer needed backup and only looked at the map when there was a change in the schedule to change his stopping times.

Ben met Jeremiah during the first week of school. They were both born on November 11, though Jeremiah was three years older. They hit it off instantly. Ben still four feet ten inches, Jeremiah six feet one inch. They were inseparable. So much so that anything Jeremiah was invited to do, Ben received an invitation to also.

By the end of September, he had been invited to attend his first party at the home of an upperclassman for Halloween. He was very excited, and I was thrilled for him. He knew that he wanted to attend the party as his favorite band's lead singer, which necessitated purchasing a dreadlock wig.

The wig was expensive, and he agreed to pay for half of it. While taking it home, he commented that the locks were too long and discussed cutting them. I told him that neither of us knew how to cut hair, and the locks would unravel if he did so. I also told him not to do it.

Days before the party, I noticed that it had been cut, and the outcome was as I had expected. The areas that were cut had come unraveled. Ben had stopped cutting when he realized that I had been right, but the damage was already done. I walked out of his bedroom, walked to the telephone in mine, and called my dad to ask him to talk to me until the desire to cause Ben harm passed.

My dad chuckled and then listened as I reasoned through what I would do next. The issue was not whether he deserved to go to the party or not. That decision was made by his new friends, and he deserved to attend from the moment he was invited. The issue was not whether he loved me or not. Adolescents do not cease to love their parents when they decide to try things on their own.

The issue was the condition of the wig. I went to Ben and we sat to talk. I told him what I had reasoned out when on the telephone with his grandfather (transparency) and reminded him that I had specifically told him not to cut the wig (boundaries). We agreed that he had cut the wig for which we had both paid half and in so doing ruined my half as well. He then was expected to reimburse me for my half. He found someone to do some repairs to the wig and had a wonderful time at the party.

The high school that he attended had an arts day in the month of December. During this day, all of the students would get a chance to go to any of the classrooms that were devoted to the arts and participate in some of the activities. There were various art projects and mediums. There were

Wendy Morse

activities to celebrate the engineering discoveries made by artists. The music room was open with all of the instruments at everyone's disposal.

It was into the music room that Ben wandered and picked up a trumpet. The music teacher heard him play and would not let him leave the room until he joined the band. It took some rearranging of his schedule, but it was worth it. The teacher was enthusiastic, talented, and optimistic. From that time until he graduated from college, I never saw him without an instrument in his hand.

Music is one of those experiences that must be learned sequentially. Ben found comfort not just in the playing and learning of a new piece but also in learning how to play different instruments. He knew that no matter what else he had to learn that day, the music would come easily because there was only one way to teach it.

The band played in concerts and competitions, and I watched while my son became his own person. At the beginning of the school year, he was Jeremiah's friend. Now he was Ben. When I dropped him off at school in the morning, many people said hello to him and would wait for him to catch up to walk in with him. When I went to the school for any reason, I discovered that we had also, quite seamlessly, moved from being Wendy's son to me being Ben's mom.

He was getting taller rapidly, and I had noticed that he had stains on the front of his shirts every day. I asked him about all of the spilling he seemed to be doing. Without skipping a beat, he reported that his mouth was not in the same place from one day to the next depending on how much he had grown. He went on to say that I was the one that taught him about his spatial relationship difficulties, and this was a clear example of them.

This was also true when he was fitted for the suit he was to wear in his uncle's wedding. We ordered the suit and went for the fitting when it arrived. I had him wear the shoes he would be wearing for the wedding. The person doing the fitting attempted to shorten the pants to fit for the moment. The wedding was two months away, and I was trying to get him to leave the pants a little long. I told the man that Ben was growing as we spoke and finally convinced him to leave them a little long. Two months later, they were a perfect fit. Two months after that, they were too short.

When spring came, he prepared to join the track team with Jeremiah. There were only the two of them on the boys' team, and they enjoyed the time together. They became co-captains, which was something of a joke until the following school year when there were more guys on the team. Ben and Jeremiah would be co-captains of the track and cross country teams through the spring of 2001. After Jeremiah graduated, Ben became captain until his graduation in June of 2003.

Ben also learned how to play the guitar and bass guitar while in high school. He found and dated a wonderful young lady for three years. He made many friends and learned about his desire to take care of some of the people that complicated their own lives with the decisions they made.

Everyone was welcome at our home, and I made no allowances for the expectations that I had with his friends. The rules that I had for Ben applied to everyone, as did the patience. I could leave anything out without worrying about it being stolen. I remember one weekend that I had the rent in cash laying on a table next to the front door, and none of the kids going in and out touched it. My parents were surprised at this, and I just shrugged. I had expected nothing less.

Wendy Morse

During the summer between his freshman and sophomore years, he and Jeremiah spent a lot of time together. This included days when I was at work. One time, I got home before Ben did and realized I didn't know enough about what they were doing during the day to know where he was. I waited somewhat impatiently for his return. He arrived home with Jeremiah an hour later, by which time I was ready with what I would say. I let them know that I understood Jeremiah's freedom, as he was about to be a senior, had a third degree black belt in Tae Kwon Do, and knew the neighborhood very well. This was not true of Ben. He was responsible for his own safety whenever he left my home, and the best I could hope for was to know where he was and what he was wearing so I could identify the body. From then on, whenever Ben left the house, he left a note with a list of the places and times he was going to be throughout the day, as well as what he was wearing.

The high school was located within a college campus, and the students that performed well enough academically were allowed to take college courses. These were not advanced placement courses but actual college courses with other college students. Ben took one each year and thoroughly enjoyed them. By the time he graduated from high school, he had one semester completed at the college level with a 4.0 average.

By his senior year, he was five feet eleven inches, captain of the track and cross country team, had the same girlfriend since his sophomore year, was a member of the National Honor Society, and everyone stopped to talk to him as he entered the school. I watched him live by the example of his best friend, Jeremiah, as he made a point of befriending a freshman every year. He was sought out by teachers to complete needed tasks in the school, sought out by friends when they needed advice, and approachable by anyone else that needed to know something he knew. He was working part time as a peer advocate with a program that had clients with mental health and developmental needs, and he was there for them whenever he could be.

This was a time of some larger, difficult issues. He was making decisions that he did not always share with me until after the fact. This was to be expected as he was getting older and there was no way to tell me everything of his life over the course of a day. Many of the decisions I will probably never know. There was one occasion when he shared a decision he had made after days of agonizing guilt.

He reported that he and his girlfriend had sex. He had been worried about how this would affect his relationship with his girlfriend. He had worried about how this would affect his relationship with me since I had often spoken of waiting until he was older. He was worried that he had not thought ahead about the consequences of his decision.

In a short time it was determined that the decision did not result in pregnancy. Both remained healthy with no sexually transmitted diseases. The issue of his guilty feelings remained. These feelings proved helpful in warding off a repeat of the decision.

It is not that I wanted to use guilt as a means to control Ben's behaviors. Guilt is a part of moving toward personal responsibility. Not in the way we sometimes use it to get our children to do things they don't want to do like getting them to help out around the house by always talking about how hard we work. This guilt was about feeling like he had betrayed my trust. This guilt was about feeling like he had betrayed her trust. It was also the kind of guilt we feel when we have done something we know to be wrong and the consequences are personal and internal instead of external.

As difficult as it was to hear him tell this story, it was good to know that he was taking personal responsibility. Even in the absence of external consequences he had learned a lesson about the damage that can be done to self esteem in the face of a bad decision.

It was during this time that I realized how much it hurt me to know that my child could make such a bad and painful decision. I struggled with not saying and doing things that would be for the purpose of hurting him back. Hurtful words like "you think you're better or smarter than me?" and "you'll never amount to anything if you keep making decisions like that" were running through my mind. Instead we talked things through and later I was glad that I had kept calm. He had enough regret to carry without having to carry my regret heaped upon him through harsh words.

The truth is that I do want him to be better and smarter than me. I want him to accomplish things far beyond what I have accomplished. I want to be proud to know him and be part of his life. Telling him that he is capable of making better decisions and that I believe he is destined for bigger and better things seems a more likely way of achieving it than telling him the opposite. No matter how much influence his friends, girlfriend, or own thought processes had, my words could have an immeasurable effect.

While his decision making continued to improve the learning difference he had continued to annoy him as he tried to learn things that seemed easy for everyone else. Let me just interject a few words about driving lessons. I had taught him most of what he needed to learn. I knew it would be difficult with his spatial relationship difficulties, but when he came to a stop at the first corner with his own body parallel to the stop sign and the front of the car sticking out into the middle of the intersection, it became very clear that we needed a patient professional. Thank goodness they exist. Thank goodness they have dual mechanical controls. (He drives very well.)

To the outside world, everything was as perfect as it could be. I was the only one that had direct knowledge of how severe things could get for him when the anxiety disorder and unresolved feelings of the abuse intertwined with one another. There were continued times of extreme anxiety, and we could talk those through. He once told me that anxiety could be best described as being in a room with one hundred people—ninety-nine of them like you, and you will spend the entire night worrying about the one that doesn't. At these times, I would ask him at what point another person's opinion of him began to matter more than his own. There were times when he struggled with memories of the sexual abuse and attended counseling to deal with how the abuse affected his relationship with his dad.

Approximately three times a year, Ben experienced a huge breakdown. The warning signs came once he was in the middle of one. He would raise his voice, swear, and threaten. Anyone that knew him did not believe it got that bad, and it did not get that bad in anyone else's presence when he was in high school. It looked like he was going to add a rage disorder to the list.

When they occurred, I always had the same response. I would tell him that he could call me anything he wanted, swear, and threaten, but as long as he stopped yelling, then I would know that he did not need to go to the hospital. After a few minutes of this, I would ask him to remove the swearing. After a few minutes more, he would be asked to stop the threatening. Finally, I expected him to sit down. Step by step and with purpose, we would end these hostilities as quickly

Wendy Morse

as we could. He would then increase his medication for three to seven days until the level of attendant anxiety reduced and then return to normal dose until the next event.

Like so many other parents, I was always so relieved when they were over that I did not go back to talk about them later. Just let it go was what I thought. As he matured, they happened less, and I thought he might grow out of them entirely.

We had learned that certain things were necessary to keep his life in balance. Music, friends, family, running, medication, and reading were all a part of this balance. I started to go to church again and found a United Methodist Church that I did not think was going to close. I convinced him to go with me on a Mother's Day. By this time, he was too disinterested. His hair was all the way down his back, and the things I listed earlier were his primary focus. There were no other kids his age in the church either. I suppose it didn't help when one of the children handing out flowers to all of the mothers in the congregation thought he was a woman.

By the time I found a church with kids his age that had different bands that played on Sundays and would have known he was becoming a man, he was getting ready for college. He wanted to spend every waking moment in preparation for moving to Boston, Massachusetts.

It was his aunt Colleen that introduced him to the Berklee College of Music in Boston, Massachusetts. From the moment he set foot on the campus in his junior year of high school, he was hooked, and nothing could dissuade him. We had already gone to one of the state schools in New York that had a well known music department.

It was their open house, and Ben had waited patiently in line for the opportunity to speak to the head of the music department. He asked about their program and if they had courses in contemporary music. The department head saw that he was dressed nicely but had long hair, and he took on a condescending tone. He told Ben that he would have to audition and asked what instrument he would play. His favorite instrument was the bass guitar, so he said that would be his audition instrument. This further annoyed the department head, and he looked his nose down on Ben even further and indicated that this was not an appropriate instrument for their school. Ben replied that he could have chosen trumpet or classical guitar, but now they would never know, would they. It was their audition, and they failed miserably.

The Berklee College of Music welcomed him with open arms. My brother Michael and sister-in-law Colleen also welcomed him with open arms. They lived not far from Boston and would be there for him for any need he might have. We begged and borrowed to get the money for him to start. We managed to acquire all of the things on the list that dorm students were expected to have. He packed, he planned, he prepared, I prayed. After all, "this adolescent belonged to the Father."

Letting Go

Moving day. I don't know why people call it moving *day*. Moving has always seemed to take weeks whenever I have done it. Yet here we were, smack dab in the middle of moving day.

There is not much that I remember of the day. He was seventeen years old and acting like he was ready. There were stairs to climb and stuff to carry and settle. He had two roommates to meet and their parents. The first of the two, Justin, had been there long enough to settle in, and I liked his mother. The second came after Ben had settled, and he and his parents brought a feeling of discomfort with them.

He found where to sign in, and—miracle of miracles—he was enrolled and expected. I found my way to the parent orientation and—miracle of miracles—managed to sit through it and not get up and scream, "This is all a mistake; I'm not ready yet." I learned that I needed to give my son written permission to secure his own medical care and did so before we parted. I learned his address and telephone number and made promises to keep in touch.

The day also included trips to the college bookstore for souvenirs (my father had accidentally purchased a child-sized hat for Ben that ended up fitting my sister-in-law perfectly), large crowds of people, and going out to dinner. There were times that Ben and I looked at each other, and it was as if we were the only two people alive as we tried to freeze time. Perhaps he was trying not to yell, "This is all a mistake; I'm not ready yet."

Then I remember it was time to say good-bye. I was armed with the written directions I needed to get out of Boston and going in the right direction to get home. Let's just say that it was a good thing that I had listened closely to the directions as they were written because I could not see anything through the veil of tears that flooded my eyes as I drove away. While there is nothing I would do to change the decision to leave, I still cry when I remember that day.

The early telephone reports from school were mixed. He really liked one of his roommates, Justin, and the other one was high all of the time and never went to class. That roommate was only there for one semester, and his replacement was older and kept to himself.

There was a mouse that ran through their dorm room a few times. Ben decided to ask the dorm director if there was a policy regarding the treatment of the rodent. The director explained that these rodents were plentiful because Boston was in the middle of the construction project affectionately known as the "Big Dig." (This is a project to move all vehicle traffic in Boston underground, and it was displacing a number of rodents.) Ben asked if he could have a cat, to which the director replied, "No pets." Ben then pointed out that they were letting him have a mouse. The director was not amused.

He and some friends had decided to go somewhere that required train travel. They went to the Green Line and were passing a homeless man on the platform. The man was saying hello to them, but they ignored him, as they had been instructed during one of their orientations. The man got up and grabbed Ben and slammed him against a railing and said, "We aren't happy with you right now."

Ben told me that he instantly remembered two stories that I had told in which it was important to know that anyone calling themselves *we* has the strength of more than one person. The other was that of a parent who arrived at my office screaming and threatening. In that story, I had explained to him that the threat wasn't to me but rather something that this parent was feeling. When I acknowledged that she was feeling threatened because of something I had done and we figured out a way of fixing it, she was fine.

Based on this information, he looked down at the man and said, "I'm not going to fight with you. Do you feel better now?" The man paused and stared at him. He said it again, and this time the man loosened his grip a little. By this time his friends had noticed his predicament and took his lead. They stood nearby and told the man everything was okay. Ben finally said that he was sorry if the man thought he had become invisible because they had ignored him and that the next time he saw the man he would say hello. The man let him go and said thank you.

He was not prepared for the breakup with his longtime girlfriend from high school. He wasn't gone that long before she started to see someone else. She broke up with him over the phone in September, and then at Thanksgiving they decided to talk. I took him to see her, and when he got back in the car after their conversation, he told me that she had revealed that she had never loved him but that she liked how she felt to be with someone that was so well liked and popular in school. He moaned and said it was bad enough that they had broken up and now he had to feel bad retroactively to when they first started to date. I felt very badly for him, but sometimes it was hard to keep a straight face when he made observations like that.

Not far into the year, I came home to eight messages on my answering machine. It was a running account of his day. When I listened, they went as follows:

"Mom, I just passed out as I was going to the bathroom; this does not seem normal, so I am going to the doctor."

"Mom, the doctor thinks I have a kidney stone. She gave me some pain medication and some coffee filters and said to go to the hospital if the pain gets worse."

"Mom, the pain is worse, and I'm going to the hospital. I've called Uncle Michael and Aunt Colleen too."

"Mom, I'm at the hospital and waiting to be seen; nothing in the filter so far."

"Mom, Uncle Michael is on his way, and the doctors are going to run some tests."

"Mom, I'm waiting for the results of tests and Uncle Michael."

"Mom, Uncle Michael is here, and we are both waiting for the results of the tests."

"Mom, aren't you ever coming home?"

I called immediately, and he had found out that he had most likely passed the stone in the morning, which was why it had hurt so bad he passed out. His uncle Michael had bought him a pizza and was driving him back to his dorm. We agreed to talk later. The next day, he told of how his doctor had asked if he had pain leading up to the stone passing. He had told her that he felt it but thought it was a side stitch because he had been running a lot. At this point, she took his face in her hands and said, "Honey, if it hurts, there is something wrong." He also reported that his friends in the dorm were in awe that he had a kidney stone and wanted to hear everything about it when he returned.

The other big story of his freshman year involved his faith. He reported that he had started to attend church with a friend. The services took place on the second floor of a church where the leader had rented space. I listened as week after week he reported on the activities and things that the leader had said. As I began to question the program, he reported that the leader had told him that I would do so and to be ready. He further reported that many of the program participants had little contact with their families, and he had told the leader that wouldn't happen to us because I trusted him.

My parents looked up the program online and found that it was a cult. The leader had been a licensed psychologist in another state and was facing charges due to unethical and illegal contact with his clients. I had to pick my words carefully. This man had prepared my son for my objections, and I risked losing him to this program. I called Ben and offered to come to Boston to meet this man who had such an influence in his life. I said that this might be a program I would like to join and provided him with the words that I wanted him to use when telling this man I was coming.

When the leader's response was to avoid meeting me, it opened a door through which I could talk to Ben about the mixed messages he was getting and encouraged him to do his own research. He found the same information we did, and it was a good thing that I was able to go to see him quickly because it really upset him that he could be so vulnerable.

We talked about what made him vulnerable and that was the need for some type of spiritual connection. We talked about ways he could recognize these types of lies earlier in a relationship. Mostly, we talked about what would happen if he could not convince his friend to leave also and he would have to leave him behind. This was not the first time we had left others behind and had to trust that the Father had a plan. It was no easier than the first. But the plan was still not ours to manipulate, and letting go was something we needed to do again.

Things were quieter for the remainder of the year. He joined a heavy metal band, was invited to move into an apartment with men that would be juniors and seniors the following year, and got through the year with a 3.8+ average. Not too shabby.

Moving day. He had spent most of the summer with his aunt and uncle so that he could first find a job near where he was going to live and then work there. He was moving in with four men over the age of twenty-one, and he was eighteen. They had asked him when their first choice backed out, but it was a great compliment nonetheless. The city of Boston is full of people looking for roommates, they chose him because they wanted him.

He was not the first person to move in that day, and one of the parents was already busy in the kitchen setting things up and telling the men what to do. Aunt Colleen and I helped Ben bring his things in. This included a large haul from Costco so no one would have to worry about paper products, light bulbs, or a small tool kit.

The mother in the kitchen was talking about taking everyone to the grocery store because the nearest one was so far away. Ben was working at the nearest grocery store, which was less than half a mile away, and I let her know. She asked if I was sure. I ignored her. There were many comments that I ignored while her husband just rolled his eyes behind her back. Among the things that I did hear was that she had just dropped her youngest off at college and that made it easier for me to understand her flurry of activity and once again just let it go.

After moving Ben's things in, I prepared to say good-bye, and this mother actually asked why I wasn't staying to help him get settled. Aunt Colleen beat a hasty retreat to the front door, the mother's husband snuck out of the kitchen, and the young men all headed for their rooms, as it was clear I had heard enough and planned to respond. I simply told her that my son was capable of setting up his own space and I had enough respect to let him do so.

Earlier in the move, she had asked me to write down my name, address, and telephone number in case any of the parents needed to contact one another. I had written my name and address. As I left, I gave it to her, and she said that I had forgotten to write my telephone number. I told her I had not forgotten and left.

I called Ben later to see if he was settled. He told me he was all set. He also told me that he was grateful that I was not like that other mother but that she had redeemed herself by filling the house with food and taking everyone out to dinner.

Then it happened. He was carrying a full academic load, working part-time, and living off campus. It had been well over a year, but he was clearly having a meltdown when I was on the telephone with him one evening. I started to use my usual technique from a distance, and his response was to tell me that I was too "****ing far away to do anything about it." I told him that far does not mean what he thinks it means and was there within seven hours.

We arrived at my brother's home very late that night. Ben was still swearing and yelling because I had decided to ask only that he get in the car and put his seat belt on before driving. My brother had never seen him act this way before, and while he had more years of experience in the field working with adolescents with mental health issues, he was not prepared for what he witnessed. I could tell from his face that he was torn between providing a professional response and wanting to deck this kid who was talking to his sister this way.

I motioned for my brother to give us time, and I had Ben stop yelling then stop swearing then stop threatening and then sit down. We made it through the night, and this time I was determined that we would talk and resolve this issue. After he took an increased dose of his medication in the morning, I started the discussion. It was then that I learned that these had all been psychotic breaks. He had no memory of any of them, and it was time for professional intervention.

We had heard about EMDR, which stands for Eye Movement Desensitization Reintegration. Very simply put, the premise is that when someone experiences a trauma, the two hemispheres of the brain stop talking to each other. This usually results in the person having an intense emotional response to the event or a completely analytical response to the event. Through the use of traditional therapy, combined with eye movement, a person can begin to reintegrate the event and experience some resolution of the event.

It was also unclear how much of the event Ben remembered. After he attended a few sessions through the counseling center at the Berklee College of Music, the therapist helped him find someone in Boston who was a licensed therapist that also was trained in hypnotherapy and EMDR. Ben had remembered almost all of the abuse, so hypnotherapy was not necessary. He was asked if he had ever dissociated, and when it was explained to him, he recalled that he had done so once during the time span of the abuse, but he found it no better to watch than endure, so he wouldn't allow it to happen again.

During the first couple of months of treatment, he sounded terrible. The safety plan was that he had the ability to call the therapist day or night after being given his office number, cell phone number, and a home number. I added having him call me every day to make sure he was all right. He spoke of waking in the morning and being surprised to see a man's face staring back at him in the mirror. He spoke of feeling like he was vulnerable to everyone as he struggled to get past this therapy that took him back to being three years old.

Slowly but surely, he became stronger. He talked about the abuse as though it were finally over. He recognized that he was stronger than he thought at the time but that didn't mean he was strong enough to stop it. He picked up everything that had been in the closet in his heart that he had built as a child. He looked at it from all angles. He kept what was good and discarded what was not wanted. He was finally able to let go of the little boy that haunted his every moment with uncertainty and fear.

A couple of months later, he called me to tell me that he was having one of the worst anxiety attacks of his life, but it was no big deal because for the first time it wasn't laced with fear, doubt, rage, and regret. He said that he simply talked out loud to himself until the feeling passed and finally felt like a true Bostonian as well. It was then that I learned that he had stopped taking his anxiety medication. He is still medication free.

Moving day. (Everyone moves on the first of September in Boston.) The place was blocks from Fenway Park, the Charles River, and his college campus. It was his junior year.

The heavy metal band he was in was doing gigs in the Boston area that he set up. Most were in bars that he could not be in when he was not playing. They wrote songs and practiced together. It was always fun to see them play when I went to visit.

Ben was well into his major as a music therapist and enjoying everything that he learned. Whatever else may happen in his life, there is no doubt that he will be serving others.

In December of 2005, it finally happened. After years of praying and hoping, Ben watched the movie *The Chosen*. I gave him the book to read, as well as *My Name is Asher Lev*, also by Chaim Potok. He was completely enthralled with this message of his heritage. He remembered that I had tried to introduce him to the Messianic Jewish community in Buffalo when he was twelve, but he was not interested. Now he couldn't wait to find out more about it.

He found a Messianic Jewish temple to attend and immediately began the process for Bar Mitzvah. While carrying a full schedule at school and working part time, he now added taking Hebrew lessons and courses in being Jewish. We spoke all of the time of scriptures, heritage, and traditions. We prayed, and I found out about all of the things he missed not knowing as he grew up. All of the items he needed to practice his faith were provided by the grace of the Father as he began the path he was always destined to take.

It was during this time period that he got his third kidney stone. I received the call late one day, and this time it required surgery to remove. I had asked my dad to go with me, and my mother was making arrangements for us to leave and drive through the night. Ben was safely at the hospital for the night, and they were not going to do the surgery until they could stop his fever. I reminded her of the rule to sleep when he sleeps from when he was a baby, and we agreed to go the next day.

He went through the surgery well. When the doctor told him that he needed to drink more water to keep from getting them again, he stopped at every drinking fountain on his way out of the hospital and said he was never going to get one again. He somehow managed to get a 4.0 average that semester anyway.

At the end of his junior year, he and his roommate decided to remain in the same place, so we didn't have to move that year. He had found a new job that made more money. He had a new woman in his life that was instrumental in his spiritual growth. Every day brought him closer to the Father and further involvement in the temple he attended.

There were still some periodic reminders of his past. He called me at 2:00 a.m. to tell me about an incident that had happened in the park along the Charles River. He described having met an older gentleman while out walking, and they had sat and talked for hours about everything. After a time, the gentleman asked if Ben could tell he had been hitting on him. Ben still had some difficulty reading the subtle nonverbal cues of others and said he had not noticed. He went on to say that he was flattered but not interested.

When he called me, it was to express the concern that if this man had been a different person, he might have been in danger. I said that if Ben had been a different person, he might have called to say he had met a great guy but he was too old. This caused Ben to laugh. I went on to remind Ben that his now six-foot-one-inch-adult body could protect itself. He agreed and was calmer.

Throughout his time in college we wrote letters to each other for Valentine's Day. The letters were about the things we liked and appreciated in each other. They were elaborate thank-you notes, and they brought to writing the most significant events in our times apart as well as our times together. I remember that I had written to him in his sophomore year that I had finally realized why my heart broke every time that we said good-bye to each other. It was because there needed to be room for all of the pride I was going to feel at his accomplishments.

Every Mother's Day, I received a CD. These CDs contained spoken thoughts about his relationship with me. They usually included songs that he had learned on various instruments. They included songs he has written and songs that he liked that he knew I would like. I will treasure them always as a reminder of all of the work we put into making this the best relationship it could be because "this young adult belonged to the Father."

He Belongs to the Father

As he approached his senior year, he prepared us for the Bar Mitzvah. We were all so pleased with the decisions that he was making about his spiritual life that we couldn't wait to be a part of it. I was asked to read the English versions of the scriptures for that day, which was to be on his twenty-first birthday. The New Testament reading included Matthew 3:17, and I choked through the words "this is my Beloved Son in whom I am well pleased."

This was not the last time I would cry that day as the rabbi stood to speak. When he said the words, "Today, you are a man," it was just the beginning of what he needed to say of Ben. He spoke of Ben being a leader of men and the Father's plans for him. I had spent my life knowing that my son was different, knowing that he was special, knowing that he has a place to fill. Hearing the rabbi confirm what I knew to be true was an incredible affirmation.

By the close of his senior year, he had made arrangements to complete his internship in music therapy at a place that hired him full-time upon completion of the course. He had an opportunity to be part of the liturgy at the temple, which included being a third cantor for the community. He had a 3.8+ grade point average. He was ready for the next step of his life.

We went to the graduation. Upon arrival, there was a long line to enter, and we got in it. I was overhearing small bits of conversation from the woman in front of us, and she turned out to be the mother of Justin, one of Ben's first roommates. She would be the first parent I met on his first day at Berklee and the first woman I met on his last day. How amazing is that?

He graduated. He walked the stage. He met The Edge from U2, who was receiving an honorary doctorate that day. He was walking on air, and he deserved every good moment of the day.

It has been more than two years since he graduated. He has, of course, moved twice. He completed his internship and contract for full-time employment and has since moved back to Boston. He is working as a relief staff for group homes that house seriously and persistently mentally ill clients. He really enjoys the work.

He attends the temple in his community regularly and serves them as cantor, chairperson of the liturgy committee, and meets a number of other liturgical needs during the services.

His faith in the Father has grown by leaps and bounds, and every conversation we have includes what we have learned since our last conversation about our relationship to Him. Every move he makes is designed for him to achieve all of the things his rabbi said on his twenty-first birthday. His community is offering every opportunity for him to achieve these goals as well.

The expectations for the position he will hold in the community once he completes his master's degree are quite rigorous. The community is preparing him to meet the challenges of a leader through their expectations of him now. Even though Ben sometimes has doubts about how his life will turn out, they do not. The community will not rest, or let him rest, until he does.

There is a wonderful young woman in his life that is talented, strong, and supportive. He speaks of her with love, respect, and awe. He is often surprised that she feels the same way about him.

The rough times still sometimes come. There is no shortage of unwanted situations in anyone's life. The amount of time it takes to return to balance is less each time. You will be happy to know that he still laughs in his sleep.

We have come all this way to stand on the brink of a new beginning. His current life is like watching a cocoon. He is surrounded by friends and family that love him. He is supported by a community that trusts him. He is protected by the Father that owns him.

I cannot see the butterfly he is to become. I cannot guess at all what this next part of his life has in store. I cannot fathom how I was blessed to play the small part in his life that I did. All I really know is that "this man belongs to the Father."

Afterword

This book has been insistent. Whether it is published or not, the writing of it was necessary. There have been many more sleepless nights since I began, as I would suddenly awake with a number of thoughts that I would write down in outline form on a notepad I kept within arm's reach at all times.

The task of writing seemed to be the most overwhelming part of this process. The overwhelmed feeling that I had when I started to write was increased substantially when I was told it would be published. This amount increased exponentially as I neared completion of the first full draft that would go to the publisher. I have a feeling it will be a good thing that others will be the driving force from here, or I would be too overwhelmed to continue.

It has been clear in the writing of these pages that I relied heavily upon the Father all of my life, especially when I didn't know that I was. Even now I am acutely aware of the inspiration (divine influence) that infuses these words and pages. It is not that the Father has given me divine wisdom. It is rather that I will sometimes stay out of His way while His work is being done. Just as Ben needed everything to be in sequence the Father made sure that everything we needed as a family came in sequence.

Ben called me one evening to tell me that everyone he knew could not wait until the book was finished so they could read it. He was telling everyone that I was going to be a published author. He said that they would all ask the same question at some point, which was, "What is the book about?" He said he always felt like twenty minutes would pass before he would get up the courage to say it was about raising him. I told him that as excited as I was about completing the book, I too felt hesitation at telling people it is about us. Not because I do not want people to know our story, but because it feels self-centered to publicize it. Then what is the point of having a story like this one if not to share and gain from the telling?

This story is about not allowing outside influences to determine the outcome of your life. There were ways in which others let me know that I should be concerned about how Ben's life would turn out given the issues he faced. Sometimes it was in the way some people expressed pity at finding out about his experiences. At other times it was spoken outright about how he would be expected to struggle his whole life and that I needed to be ready to take care of him far into adulthood. You could almost see the outcome they pictured in their heads and the lines within which we would be forced to live no matter what choices we made from here.

Perhaps it was our stubborn streak that made us do things differently. Perhaps it was his survival in those early moments in his life that forced me to see beyond the lines. Maybe someday I will know the full influence of the divine interventions that took place in our lives as we lived them. All I know is that there are no lines that bind us to travel a certain path and I am grateful to those that said there were so I could refuse to follow them. I am grateful to those that said there weren't so that we were supported in our efforts to succeed.

This is for the "dads" in his life that gave of themselves in ways that would greatly enhance his life. My dad gave him patience, integrity, honesty, loyalty, and commitment.

His dad's dad gave him encouragement, critical thinking, self esteem, and kindness. His dad gave him life, appreciation, care, and love. His uncle Michael gave him humor, music, selflessness, and principals. He has found a way to expand the number of "dads" in his life and has chosen well.

This is for the "moms" in his life that also gave of themselves to greatly enhance his life. My mom gave him the ability to learn, generosity, optimism, and responsibility. His dad's mom gave him attention, global thinking, self care, and laughter. His aunt Temma gave him excitement, knowledge, spontaneity, and balance. His aunt Colleen gave him a future, openness, passion, and grace. The "moms" that he has added to his life will further his growth and strength.

This is for each of you for taking the time to reach this point in our story. There will be much more to it as we continue to live our lives. There will be much more to it as people begin to share their similar stories with us from which we may all learn. There will be much more to it as people begin to tell one another their stories and grow from the giving and receiving of them. Thank you one and all.

It is going to hurt, they said, but it is the most promising pain. We strive to bring this story back to life in a way that it can be woven into the lives of all it touches, and when all is said and done, "this book belongs to the Father."